True

When Whispered

Also by Paul L. Escamilla

Longing for Enough in a Culture of More

True

When Whispered

hearing God's voice
in a noisy world

PAUL L. ESCAMILLA

ABINGDON PRESS / NASHVILLE

TRUE WHEN WHISPERED
HEARING GOD'S VOICE IN A NOISY WORLD

Copyright © 2010 by Abingdon Press

This book is printed on acid-free paper.

Library of Congress Cataloging-in-Publication Data

Escamilla, Paul L.
  True when whispered : hearing God's voice in a noisy world / Paul L. Escamilla.
    p. cm.
  ISBN 978-1-4267-0299-0 (pbk. : alk. paper)
  1. Spiritual life—Christianity. 2. Quietude. 3. Listening—Religious aspects—Christianity.
4. Prayer—Christianity. I. Title.
  BV4501.3.E828 2010
  248—dc22

                                                                    2009052477

10 11 12 13 14 15 16 17 18 19—10 9 8 7 6 5 4 3 2 1

MANUFACTURED IN THE UNITED STATES OF AMERICA

To

Fred B. Craddock

and

Don E. Saliers

teachers in classroom and
sanctuary of things true when whispered

Contents

Part I. *The practice of prayer*

Part II. *Habits of the heart*

Part III. *Whispering in the world*

Contents

Acknowledgments

Every time I go about the writing task I find myself both alone and very much accompanied. Since home is my primary setting for such undertakings, our three children swirl in and out of the writing process in delightful ways that both distract me from my work and deepen me in it. My wife, Elizabeth, provides a constant, lambent presence, coupling the gift of encouragement with the keenest of insights. My parents, as ever, are near, even from a distance.

Nancy Watson has offered invaluable assistance with this particular writing project, from proofing to source-checking to offering suggestions regarding style and phrasing. Rhonda Huser has secured permissions and assisted with other inquiries. Barry Webster has given his time in reflective conversation on the subject of the book, as have Glen Spears and Robin Lovin; Ted Butler and Anna Hosemann-Butler have generously offered a place apart in a setting that somehow has the effect of silencing, then steadying, my pen.

Perkins School of Theology at Southern Methodist University, where I currently serve, has been more than a theological school; it has proven to be, in the very best sense, a community seeking God, and I am privileged to share that pilgrimage. My supervisor, Roberta Cox, holds a special regard for the written word and the crafted sentence, and has thereby heightened my own. Kathy Armistead at Abingdon has provided just the right measure of guidance and support. Finally, First United Methodist Church Richardson, Texas, our family's church home, has, through a liminal season, opened its doors to us through Word, sacrament, and community, and we have been grateful to belong.

Many others populate these pages, and have accompanied my writing task—more even than I realize. We are for a lifetime beholden to those who love us in either forgotten or unseen ways, beginning with God, and who, beyond our awareness, follow us in the form of goodness and mercy all the days of our lives. Their influence is more whispered than shouted, and so are they remembered here.

Ordinary Time, 2009

God at a whisper

Some things are true when whispered,
but not when shouted.
—Søren Kierkegaard

Life is growing louder. We know this without benefit of statistics. Nor is the loudening of life merely a matter of increased volume. Take away the planes, trains, and automobiles, mute the alarm clocks and cell phones, silence the lawn mowers and leaf blowers, disengage the MP3 players and televisions, the amplifiers and megaphones, the buzzers on our microwaves, dryers, and coffeemakers, and the tiny little speakers embedded in our musical greeting cards, and life would still seem louder than it once did. Life growing louder is not merely a function of decibels; it reflects the very manner in which we live.

We have become adept at taking life in snippets and sound bites rather than by savoring its gifts day-to-day and year after year. Where once we lingered before the majestic, silenced by its grandeur, a quick snapshot makes an efficient souvenir for viewing some other time. Where we used to dine, we graze; where we used to talk, we text. Where we used to read, we skim. Compact not only describes our most recent digital accomplishments, it is also what we have become with respect to sense and sensibility. We have compressed more thoughts than ever into our brains, but have done less thinking; more images, but with less seeing; more songs, but with less singing; more sound overall, but with less listening.

Yet life growing louder is not merely a function of the manner in which *we* pass through the *world*. Just as important is the manner in which the *world* passes through *us*. Overtures, solicitations, promotions, and appeals of all sorts request or require our attention morning, noon, and night. The word *advertise* means "to turn toward," and stimuli of all sorts seek just that from us—a turning of the ears, the eyes, the mind, the heart, the feet, and usually the pocketbook, toward a certain response. These appeals grow louder and bolder over time, more sophisticated in the ways they promise either to reduce or enlarge some aspect of life—to offer the grand granulated, the epic abbreviated, the sublime supersized; fears eradicated, dreams realized; ambitions materialized, complexities simplified. Mystery and wonder, dimensions of human experience once regarded as vast and inscrutable, are purported to have been captured beneath snow globes and made available for purchase.

That's advertising, and it's everywhere, appealing without pause for the branding rights to our senses, emotions, thinking, and decision-making. A slightly different word, *avert*, means "to turn away," as in "averting our gaze," a practice we learn over time in order to deflect the endless stream of appeals that rushes toward us. Throughout our lives we are involved to some degree or another in either the act of turning toward a given stimulus or away from it, toward or away, as we repeatedly make the choice for acceptance or dismissal. At the same time, of course, we are making our own overtures of whatever sort, others weighing *our* appeals in the very same way we evaluate theirs—turning toward or away, toward or away. We have become, in effect, a society of shaking heads.

The practice of averting our gaze comes at a price. Our own resistance to certain appeals, while appropriate and necessary, has effects that reach far beyond the thing resisted. There is beauty we overlook, the friendly overture we dismiss, good news of which we are automatically suspicious. Developing our capacities to deflect or downplay others' attempts to gain our attention can leave us cynical, jaded, or colorblind. When the truly genuine comes our way, how do we know it from all that *claims* to be genuine, in order to let our ears take in its music and our minds and hearts its meaning?

The effects of our experience of life growing louder are not limited to whether we pause to admire the upper ridges of a cloudbank or note the trace of weariness in a coworker's voice. In a noisy world, we stand to lose the one thing most essential for clear thinking; that is, the simple ability to *hear* ourselves thinking. As a result, we have developed the tendency to do less in the way of forming judgments of any critical sort and more in the way of making choices based on the least line of resistance. When we grow tired or strained by the volume and haste of our living, ease of use becomes more convenient than rightful use, and "what works for me" often substitutes for what is faithful for *us*. When the decisions of daily life are steeped in noise and distraction, common sense and the common good sometimes lose our allegiance, if only because they lose our attention.

Something inside us holds out hope for a better way, for journeying through our lives and our life together as something other than a society of shaking heads. We have grown weary of trading what is good for what is convenient, finding things entertaining and amusing but not particularly instructive, and seeing the numinous peddled as though it were merchandise. We have had the experience, as T. S. Eliot once put it, but missed the meaning, and now we have begun to *miss* the meaning we have missed—that awareness, thoughtfulness, and openness that would ensure a sense of depth and dimension to our living. We want to believe again what we have once either believed or wished to believe: that we do not live by volume alone; that the manner by which we go through life matters as much as the destination we have in mind; and that if we are to be truly human, mystery and wonder, or as the psalmist once said it, things too great and too marvelous for us, must be allowed to leave us awed even as we leave them unabridged.

"Some things are true when whispered," Søren Kierkegaard once observed, "but not when shouted." I think with these words the Danish philosopher was seeking to say that as life grows louder some of its richest qualities, such as goodness and honesty, gentleness and generosity, beauty and awe, tend to be drowned out in the process. These sorts of gifts do not usually employ bullhorns and battering rams for the purpose of impressing themselves upon the mind and heart; hence, they will never, in the conventional sense, compete for space in those voluntary realms. But Kierkegaard is not all about the gloom of displacement. If we turn our ear for a moment to the lefthand side of his observation, we hear him saying something considerably more hopeful: "Some things are true when whispered. . . ." There is beyond or perhaps *before* all the shouting a whisper already spoken that nonetheless waits to be heard again, waits to convey to us things so utterly trustworthy that they might well be described with a single word: true.

I wonder if Kierkegaard's saying was his own attempt to listen for that earlier whisper in the place where there had lately been only noise and haste. Perhaps he hoped that ears long inured to the shouting might suddenly turn in the direction of that whisper and hear something long forgotten, but longer remembered. I'm writing this book, I suppose, as my own way of attempting just that—to call you as the reader to listen for a whisper that quietly makes its way into the noise and haste of what is often a crowded life, hoping that you might hear that whisper somewhere beneath the clamor and turn in the direction from which it has come, as children weary with the carnival's cotton candy turn home.

If all goes well, you may find that the whisper is coming not so much from words on a page as from a voice that lies *behind* the page, or even *beyond* the page. I am speaking, of course, about God, who has been discovered countless times both behind things and beyond them—from burning bushes to stone tablets to the most pedestrian of parables. We know, for instance, that God once had the opportunity to speak in a mountain-splitting wind, then a violent earthquake, then a raging fire, and did not. Instead, behind these, or beyond them, God spoke in a still, small voice; some say it was a whisper (1 Kings 19:11-12). Just imagine it—the Sovereign of history, the Ruler of the cosmos, the God of all creation, with ready access to earth, wind, and fire, waiting these out, then conveying the intended message at a volume just a hair's breadth above silence.

When you think about it, if you have ever had what you would describe as a personal encounter with God, be it in the piney woods or at a pinewood altar, the encounter was probably very much that way—audible, but just barely. More often than not, it seems, God speaks to us at a volume that has us leaning forward, a gesture that looks for all the world like reverence, but really has more to do with trying to hear a little better. Among motives for drawing closer to God, one can do worse.

When nineteenth-century sealer James Waddell introduced Christianity and its Bible to the native Yaghan people living at the southern tip of South America, one of the natives is said to have taken the missionary's strange black book in hand, opened its pages, and placed his ear against it, having been led to understand that the God of the Christians spoke through its pages. In the chapters ahead, that is essentially what we will be doing. Having ourselves been led to believe that God speaks through the Bible, we will, in a manner of speaking, put our own ear to its pages. If we listen long and quietly enough, we may hear a whisper behind or beyond whatever silence we first experience. In that whisper we may begin to hear ourselves quietly addressed in some life-giving, life-summoning way. In my experience, holy encounter need not involve a bullhorn or battering ram. The meeting is often less like a lightning *bolt*, more like a lightning *bug*, with epiphanies of the tiniest order blinking silently before us in the interest of luring us out of our lawn chairs.

We will look at three dimensions of the life of faith, exploring ways these closely woven threads of the Christian life lead us to listen, love, and live in ways that truly matter for us as well as for the world. The three dimensions are the practice of prayer, the habits of the heart, and the ways we go about whispering in the world—that is, how we begin to lead and serve more faithfully in and through our life together. Collectively these three dimensions of who we are fold in upon one another to form the graceful matrix of understandings and practices that undergird the strange and beautiful journey we call the life of faith. Our hope is to gain some sense of the feel of each, the fit between them, and the worldview they engender as they present us with a vision of life well lived.

Every time you take up this book and read its pages, as you are doing just now, the book will, by its very design, be open to the sky, introducing one page after another to the light of day and the night's array of wonders. In turn, every page will offer whatever it has to give—at least words on a page; perhaps more. The way a book is read is also, I believe, very much the way the heart responds when held in careful hands, the hands of a true friend, for example, or maybe even God. It, too, opens to the sky, ready to offer both the treasure and turmoil of its own depths, and to accept whatever things are given in return—starlight, sunlight, manna in-between.

Maybe the heart I have just described is your own. As you hold this book in your hands, imagine that your heart is similarly held in the trustworthy hands of One who knows you plainly and loves you well. Imagine, too, that your heart is offering up whatever it holds—questions, doubts, struggles, longings, delight, reverence, trust. And then imagine it receiving those gifts that come whenever, even for a brief time, hush overtakes hurry, and the footfall of God's goodness finds its way to your heart's door: the gift of insight, or of some assurance; the gift of a sense of purpose or calling you have not known before. Perhaps the gift is nothing other than this: to be given an ear for hearing such things as are only true when whispered.

The practice of prayer

I wish to kneel where prayer has been valid.

T. S. Eliot

Chapter 1

The precariousness
of praying

They heard the sound of the LORD God walking in the garden at the time of the evening breeze, and the man and his wife hid themselves from the presence of the LORD God among the trees of the garden. But the LORD God called to the man, and said to him, "Where are you?" He said, "I heard the sound of you in the garden, and I was afraid, because I was naked; and I hid myself."
—Genesis 3:8-10

When it comes to relating to God, things have never been altogether straightforward. If our own lives are not proof enough, the Bible, from beginning to end, gives us plenty of evidence of crossed signals, missed cues, mixed motives, and misconstrued meanings in the relationship between creature and Creator. If we are looking for examples, Genesis makes a good beginning. You know the story: God walks through the garden of Eden calling for the missing pair: "Where are you?" It turns out the man and woman are among the trees, hiding "from the presence of the LORD God." Once they are summoned, however, they instantly emerge from the shadows and rejoin the relationship, explaining themselves with remarkable forthrightness. "I heard the sound of you in the garden," Adam confesses, "and I was afraid" (Genesis 3:8-10).

With that brief narrative we learn something very important about the spiritual life, namely, that the presence of God is a thing we want and ward off in just about equal measure. Adam and Eve are forerunners of the rest of us, darting beneath the dark cover of trees at the first sign of the divine, then answering immediately when they are summoned, as though relieved to have been discovered. Still dusty behind the ears, they have learned early that the experience of encountering their Creator is a complicated mixture of worry and welcome, judgment and joy.

Picture the three—Adam, Eve, and God—talking in the shadows of the garden grove, their serpentine conversation twisting from confusion to confession.

> God: Where are you?
> Adam: I hid myself.
> God: Who told you?
> Adam: The woman.
> God: What is this?
> Woman: The serpent.

We can spend a good deal of time placing blame on those who place blame. I would rather we notice the fact that, in the moment of encounter with the God of the garden, the two slowly but surely emerge from their lost-and-hiding place, cease their shuffling, and come clean. "I ate," they each acknowledge in turn. Call their confessions convoluted if you like, but call them courageous too. If they spit and sputter their way to truth and responsibility, at least they get there.

I remember a family outing to an amusement park years ago during which overcast skies suddenly opened up in an afternoon thunderstorm. Everyone in the park sought shelter from the downpour wherever it could be found—in restaurants, under awnings, beneath pavilions. A gift shop is where our family found harbor—along with what seemed like the entire population of the park. Inside the little store, we crowded into aisles of trinkets and postcards, peering out at the rain the way a hidden mouse studies a cat walking through the room. At the counter, the clerk did a brisk business in overpriced umbrellas and ponchos, selling out of both within minutes. Those so equipped bravely ventured back into the park while the rest of us, jealous of their good fortune, waited for the skies to clear. Later in the afternoon, the storm long past and the sun shining, the park was once again bustling as before. A long line snaked from the entrance to one of the most popular amusements in the park, a ride along a "river" canal in a dug-out "log" canoe. The ride's greatest attraction, as you may already know, is the expectation that on the canoe's final descent an enormous splash of water leaves the rider thoroughly soaked.

If God is the water of our entry into the spiritual life, we will take extra precautions to be certain we don't get wet, and also to ensure that we do. Adam and Eve's initial instinct is much like our own—to head for the gift shop at the first sign of a downpour. The question God asks, "Where are you?" allows that the two are both lost and hiding, which turns out to be precisely true. For some strange reason, lost and hiding go together like axle grease and road grime, one attracting the other. This couple wastes no time in pairing the two. Having become lost through the lure of the serpent, they choose to hide rather than seek to be found.

God's first call is a question, and a searching one at that: "Where are you?" Humanity's first response is a halfhearted smokescreen, followed by transparency. And so begins the

Bible's montage of the practice of prayer. Scripture will eventually give us wonderful illustrations of direct, declaratory encounters between Caller and called, clear invitation followed by ready assent. We will see fishing boats left rocking in the shallows, abandoned coins rolling across the tax table and falling into the dirt, a blind man's only cloak cast off as of no worth by a mere summons. Yet if it is a sober dose of more-often-than-not we are after, we will never do better than this first encounter. For prayer is voluntary, employing neither leashes nor lockstep marches to accomplish its aim of securing us in a relationship with God. From the first syllable of prayer and even before, we are free, like Adam and Eve, to dart or drift from the holy conversation, able at any instant to hide from the presence or feel ourselves to be lost from it. There are plenty of leafed-out trees to serve the purpose, not to mention umbrellas and ponchos. All for a price, of course.

Two words you would never expect to have any relationship to each other are actually kissing cousins. Those words are "pray" and "precarious." Both come from a root word meaning "to ask." "Precarious" describes the shaky experience of coming hat in hand to another with a concern of real importance, which is essentially also what happens in prayer. We are uncertain, unassured; there are no formulas regarding the disposition of our request, or even that our prayer will fairly represent our actual need. It is a precarious moment of absolute dependence and trust; in other words, it is a moment for divine intervention, a reality for which we have reserved the word "grace."

If you have ever wondered if you were alone in your ambivalence about putting in the time and effort to seek God's presence, wonder no more—ambivalence is a biblical tradition that runs deep and ranges wide. If you are in line for a poncho one minute and the log ride the next, you can expect a crowd at both locations. For all sorts of reasons, we are prone to resist most vehemently the very things we long for most deeply. Even when we do choose to give God the time of day, when practicing prayer in a personal way becomes an ordinary reality in our daily lives, holy encounter continues to be a tenuous arrangement. We are the newborn calf with its mother, never more content than when it is nestled at her side, yet tottering like the dickens as she works it over with her sandpaper tongue. Sometimes we seek that cleansing, caressing contact with the mother cow; other times, it seeks us. Either way, we totter; either way, we pray.

Chapter 2

Praying before we know it

[Jesus] was praying in a certain place, and after he had finished, one of his disciples said to him, "Lord, teach us to pray, as John taught his disciples." He said to them, "When you pray . . ."

—Luke 11:1-2a

Listening for God, speaking to God—these are precarious things—and yet they matter profoundly to us. Consider how many articles you have read, sermons you have heard, conversations you have had, and, of course, jokes you have listened to on the simple yet deeply mysterious subject of relating to God in prayer. Consider the ways your own prayer life has maneuvered over the years from shallows to depths and back again. No wonder Thomas Merton described the spiritual life as "starting over." It seems that when it comes to encountering God in prayer we are always beginning again, always starting over. The crumpled-up sheets of paper have long since overflowed the wastebasket as we begin the nth draft of our letter. So far, they all begin the same way: "Dear God . . ."

"Teach us to pray," the beginner-disciples once asked Jesus. And he answered, "When you pray, say . . ." (Luke 11:1). This is one of those occasions in the Gospels when we don't know whom to thank—the disciples for being honest enough to ask a question we might be afraid was too dim-witted to ask ourselves, or Jesus for treating the question with such accommodation. Imagine the disciples' conversations leading up to this question: "How can we ask him to teach us to pray? He'll think we're fools. We might as well ask, 'Teach us to lace our sandals.' The newborn knows how to draw the mother's milk, yet we don't know how to pray?" Then there are the answers Jesus might have given after the request had been made: "Teach you to pray? Are you not Israelites as I am? From the womb we have prayed—table prayers, threshold prayers, sabbath prayers, morning prayers, night prayers, wedding prayers, graveside prayers—these are our bread and drink, the very air we breathe. They are our hopes by day and our dreams in the darkness of night. Teach you to pray?"

"Yes, teach us to pray." Their request—dim-witted or not—rises like a surrender flag from the landscape of Luke's Gospel to capture the attention of every generation of Jesus' beginner-followers since, including ours. Maybe we should know better. Maybe we should have been paying better attention in Sunday school or morning worship or Bible school or summer camp, so that as grown-ups we would have no reason to ask such a seemingly elementary question. Maybe this and maybe that, but whatever the reasons, neither and none. The disciples' question is our question too.

There may be some comfort to be found in discovering that Paul the apostle is in the same boat with the rest of us. In one of his letters he writes, "We do not know how to pray as we ought" (Romans 8:26). This from someone who is known for knowing a great deal about a great number of things, and not hesitating to say so. He knows the law of Moses backward and forward. He talks about grace like it's his middle name. He knows about heaven as if he's been there—and claims he has. He holds forth with relative ease on complex theological questions such as the nature of sin, the meaning of the Cross, the hope of resurrection, the relationship of faith and works, and the mystery of becoming a new creation in Christ. He is certain about marriage, table etiquette, ritual diplomacy, and the finer points of dealing with food that has been sacrificed to idols. Paul knows a great deal about a great number of things. But in a letter to a young church that is probably asking the same question the disciples raised with Jesus and looking to Paul for answers, he acknowledges in that one very specific area his own uncertainty: "We do not know how to pray . . ."

With these simple words of confession Paul borrows the disciples' surrender flag and raises it for himself, at once revealing his own humanness and allowing for ours. And yet with the insight that surrounds those helpless words, Paul proves the extraordinary power of divine inspiration to steady even the most precariously hoisted flag: "*Likewise the Spirit helps us in our weakness;* for we do not know how to pray as we ought, *but that very Spirit intercedes with sighs too deep for words*" (Romans 8:26, italics mine). If there is deep uncertainty about prayer in the middle of the sentence, there is equally sure assistance provided by the Spirit to the left and right. In other words, in our moment of surrender, the Holy Spirit has us surrounded.

An educator at heart, Paul has created a visual aid to illustrate his point, *showing* us the answer to our dilemma by the very way he crafts his sentence on the parchment: the Holy Spirit goes before and behind us in prayer, giving heft to flimsy words, buoyancy to bottomed-out words, strength to tired words, and deep sighs where there are no words at all. Put another way, the Spirit makes a silk purse out of a sow's ear, redeeming our feeble and frustrated efforts to move our prayers out of our own rickety frames and into the presence of God, changing our sense of God's location from heaven to here. The moment we seek the presence of God, we are already *in* the presence of God. The moment we want to pray, we are already at prayer.

Our very sighs of exasperation, yearning, or surrender are themselves the coupling of the human and the divine.

Some years ago in a congregation I served, young Kristine and her mother, Barbara, played a piano duet in Sunday morning worship. Somewhat tentatively, the child began a rudimentary version of "Amazing Grace." Soon her mother, seated at her daughter's side with one arm reaching around her, began to add light accompaniment to the left and right; as she did, Kristine's own simple melody took wing. By the end of the piece, four hands had crafted a sublime rendering of the beloved folk hymn. The simple offering of a young worshiper was infused with beauty beyond its own by the gentle, enfolding presence of a mother's light touch. The two not only *performed* "Amazing Grace"; in that moment they demonstrated it.

As we struggle to pick out even the most basic notes of prayer, the Spirit, near as our own breath, begins to fill in lightly, intuitively on every side in what truly is an amazing grace. Going back now across the pages of the New Testament to Luke, we come again to that moment the disciples ask their question of Jesus about learning to pray. Notice that theirs is not really a question—it's a statement: "Teach us to pray." Look closer, and you will see that it is not really a statement, either, but a *petition*. Petition, an earnest request of some sort, is merely another word for prayer. Theirs is an expeditionary prayer, to be sure—a pair of hikers that do not know, upon entering the canyon, when or where the exit will be found. But then, isn't all prayer expeditionary? To speak the name of God or hear the voice of God is to create the path as we walk it together, never altogether certain where the next step of either traveler will come to rest.

Prayer is sometimes presented as a prescribed set of techniques, the mastery of which leads the spiritual seeker into special realms of awareness and resourcefulness. Other times we hear that prayer is an act of speaking and listening as clear and bold as trumpets on a rooftop, clarion calls to and from God that leave not an ounce of doubt or second-guessing. These models certainly have their place along the spectrum of spiritual theory and practice. But the prayer I have come to know better than these is the prayer that stands on wobbly knees, the sort that, at any moment, could buckle into the tall grass under the gritty grace of the mother's grooming tongue. It is then, as Paul and the disciples have shown us, that we have encountered the presence and power of the Holy Spirit, gentle to love us, strong to uphold. What would topple us, moreover, sustains.

If you think of yourself as unable to break through to God in any meaningful way, remember this: when we seek to find God in prayer—even *think* about doing so—we are already finding. When we ask, we are already being given. The door upon which we would knock opens before our knuckles can even reach it. The prayer room into which we then enter may be less than opulent. In fact, it may be plain, ordinary, and unadorned. But I can assure you of this: it will shelter, and it will shade. Ask God in the most provisional terms to teach you to pray, and I will show you one prayer that is already both offered and answered. Lift a finger to play the first tentative note, and there will surely be, seated on the bench beside you, a grace so present, so instrumental in the music you are making, it is often called amazing.

Chapter 3

Embrace and surrender

Likewise the Spirit helps us in our weakness; for we do not know how to pray as we ought, but that very Spirit intercedes with sighs too deep for words.
—Romans 8:26

When Paul says the Spirit helps us to pray, he doesn't mean this as an abstraction, a fuzzy description of some metaphysical mingling of the divine with the human. True to his Jewish roots, he understands the spiritual and the physical as integral to each other, and not in the way of carrots and peas in mixed vegetables but rather of flour and yeast in Grandmother's finest homemade rolls. The spiritual is intrinsic to the physical, just as the physical is inherent in all things spiritual. Together the two make for some heavenly Sunday dinners.

So when Paul says the Spirit helps us to pray, we should not be surprised by the fact that he describes this spiritual reality in a very physical way. The Spirit, he writes, helps us to pray by *sighing* through us. (Some versions translate the Greek word as "moaning.") Paul could not have identified a human gesture reflecting a wider range of physical and emotional expression. As we know, a sigh can represent a thousand different feelings. In one instance, it is a gesture of despair; in another, exhilaration. One sigh is yielded up as the weary response to the long-expected news of a loved one's death; another by a person gazing into the eyes of their beloved across the table. One sigh means joy unspeakable; another, sadness beyond words. To sigh is to lament, to languish, to lean against our own weary frame or the next nearest for steadiness against some gathering anguish that is best expressed by the Spanish word, *insoportable*, unsupportable. Yet to sigh is also to be stirred by the marvel of a setting sun or a rising moon, to sanctify a holy moment in worship, to pause before any wonder small or great that the eye has beheld, the ear heard, or the human heart conceived.

To draw into our lungs "an unusual amount of air," as the dictionary defines a sigh, is first a gathering up of whatever resides along the landscape of both inner and outer worlds. The sighing prayer begins as a beachcomber, collecting burdens and blessings, griefs and gratitudes, hurts and tears, hopes and fears. To breathe in at such depths is our way of accepting ownership of whatever awareness or emotion weighs on us just then—both those we delight in and those we wish would be carried out on the receding tide and never seen again. Before prayer is anything besides, it is an embrace of life in all its fullness and threat. It is to hold the world, even at great cost, honestly in hand.

The Spirit who sighs within us has other arenas of respiration as well. The community of faith sighs and groans, Paul tells us (v. 23), as does all of creation (v. 22). If what we first breathe in for prayer is that which lies within the small circle of our own day-to-day world—a job, a friendship, a personal decision—then eventually the prayerful sigh begins to widen to encompass the community of faith, then the wider human community, then creation, the universe, even God. One night at bedtime, our four-year-old ended his litany of "God bless . . ." prayers with one final petition: ". . . and God bless God."

The Christian life, whether at prayer or otherwise, is a life that repeatedly asks us to take a thing in hand—the hand of another person, a nation in turmoil, a natural disaster, a broken home, or a world aching for shalom. But we are also asked to make an offering of these things of which our hand has taken hold. For to cling to anything at length, whether something we cherish or something we dread, is gradually to reduce life's breadth and scope to narrowness. The word "cling" itself comes from the Old English word *clingan*, meaning to shrink or wither, a reference, in this instance, both to the thing held and the one holding it. And so the sigh shifts from breathing in to breathing out, from gathering to relinquishing, surrounding to surrendering. If embrace is acceptance, then surrender is acceptance of another sort—no longer of ownership, but of assurance. To turn the sigh from inhaling to exhaling is to yield up what matters most deeply, what we have just now embraced fully, and entrust these things to God's keeping. It is to place them with our careful hands into a hand more careful still—the hand of God. With Longfellow we say, believing it as best we can, and sighing for the rest, *Thy hand in all things I behold, And all things in thy hand. . . .*

We could say that simply allowing the Holy Spirit to pray through us is the first and final act of embrace and surrender. To participate in this gift, whether with spoken words, uttered sighs, unknown tongues, song, dance, marching, or myriad other ways is to embrace the companionship and infilling that are God's gift of breath, first given to us, then returning to its source. And to embrace that mysterious presence and power of God among us is already to surrender our lives and the world to God's grace and guiding. By the end, embrace and surrender, what we have considered two discrete acts of faith, have been sewn together, with no trace of a seam.

Acceptance and offering. Responsibility and release. Embrace and surrender. This is the ebb and flow of our lives. It is the way we love our children, relate to our friends, cherish our life partners, navigate our vocations. And it is the path of entry into the presence of God, both at the beginning, at the last, and all along the way. The prayer of sighing is, in a sense, one form of praying known as the breath prayer—breathing in as you pray one word or phrase, breathing out on another—a method of prayer as ancient as the forest and as fresh as the wind that whispers through it. Inhale . . . *This is the day the Lord has made* . . . Exhale . . . *Let us rejoice and be glad in it* . . . Inhale . . . *Let this cup pass from me* . . . Exhale . . . *yet not my will, but yours* . . . Inhale . . . *Remove this thorn* . . . Exhale . . . *My grace is sufficient for you* . . . Inhale . . . *O Lamb of God, that takest away the sins of the world* . . . Exhale . . . *grant us thy peace.* . . . Inhale . . . *Holy Spirit* . . . Exhale . . . *guide me through.*

We spend our lives, and our life together, sowing and reaping, discovering and releasing, gathering up the tears, the marvels, the anguish, the joy, and offering these to God, cherished now in their release more than when we first possessed them. This is the mystery altogether human, altogether divine, of the Holy Spirit praying through us with sighs too deep for words; the mystery of lives that have learned the effort and grace of gathering and releasing, loving and letting go, embrace and surrender.

Chapter 4

Living from elephants' tracks

When you pray, say . . .
—Luke 11:2a

I had gone to the zoo not so much to be schooled in the spiritual life as to enjoy the animals with my daughter. But there it was, just beyond the wrought iron fence separating the savanna from the sidewalk—a lesson in prayer. Elephants trudged through mud toward the hay feeder, the occasional bird following behind, making the most of the great depressions left in the elephants' wake. The sign on the fence explained: *Small creatures drink the rainwater that collects in the footprints of the elephant.* I was reminded of the metrics of prayer.

When the disciples and Jesus share a brief exchange regarding prayer in the course of his ministry, the conversation becomes enormously instructive before a syllable of Jesus' prayer is ever spoken. "Teach us to pray," they ask him. We have already explored the way in which this very appeal is itself a prayer, the Spirit's enabling work of seeking the divine through us, begun before we even knew it had started. Now we inch along to the next few words of dialogue prior to the prayer's beginning and receive an entirely different insight.

Jesus replies to the disciples' request, "When you pray, say . . ." We do not need to know a single word that follows in order to know this: Jesus and the disciples understand what the whole biblical and historical faith tradition also understand: that not only is prayer inherently teachable, it is also fundamentally transferable. My prayer can become your prayer; yours, mine. As we have done once before, let us imagine a different scenario in this opening exchange: "Lord, teach us to pray." *What? Teach you to pray? Do you think prayer can be handed from one person to another as though it were a coin, or a loaf of bread? You must find your own prayer, discover your own voice, chart your own path to God. No one else can do this for you.*

We will instantly recognize in this fabricated response familiar words and ideas affirming our individuality and self-determination. We hear such assertions often, and in many different contexts, the message behind them all being roughly the same: *You are a unique individual, free to find your own path through life; in fact, there is no other way—you must find your own path through life. I cannot teach you which of two roads to take when they diverge; how to distinguish a good story from a bad one; or what to do when you are faced with a moral dilemma. You alone must chart your course.*

In more or less direct contrast to such a philosophy of life, the entirety of the Judeo-Christian tradition teaches a different way, a way of appropriating others' spiritual patterns and life practices to our own benefit. The word *disciple* means "one who learns" or "one who trains," implying a teacher or trainer. *Followers* of Jesus *follow* Jesus. "Be imitators of me," Paul writes to the Corinthians, without a hint of arrogance (1 Corinthians 4:16). And elsewhere, "Keep on doing the things that you have learned and received and heard and seen in me" (Philippians 4:9). "For I received from the Lord what I also handed on to you," he tells the Corinthian Christians (1 Corinthians 11:23). In this last instance he is referring to the bread and cup of the Eucharist; in other words, spiritual nourishment. The biblical model for Christian living is clearly one of imitation: one learner teaching another; one disciple training another;

one follower leading another, feeding another. Imitation is not, in this context, anathema; it is the path of wisdom.

Wendell Berry once observed that poetry can be written because it *has* been written. I am quite certain that the small creatures referred to on the sign at the zoo would agree. Their very ability to live and move and have their being is contingent on elephants first living and moving and having their being (especially the "moving" part). No elephants seeking sustenance, no tracks; no tracks, no pools of rainwater; no pools of rainwater, no small creatures. Were there no spiritual pilgrims seeking God, there would be no prayers seeking God; if there were no prayers, there would be no learning of prayer.

Teach us to number our days, that we may gain a heart of wisdom, my grandmother used to pray, borrowing a verse from the psalms. Overhearing, I learned to pray those words both with her, after her, and long before I knew what they meant or from where they had originally come. I did not understand at the time that I was drinking rainwater from an elephant's track, nor that she was doing the same. An ancient, time-kept prayer was providing sustenance for an old woman and a young child, beholden creatures both.

Bless this food to our use, and us to thy service, we ask for Christ's sake. Amen. From this mealtime prayer my grandfather never varied, and his grandchildren have drawn nourishment from it well beyond his lifetime. When visiting a cousin decades after my grandfather's death, we gathered at her table for a meal, and she led us in prayer. "Bless this food to our use, and us to thy service, we ask for Christ's sake. Amen." Did I say she led us in prayer? Better to say we both *followed* in prayer.

As we grow in faith and the practice of prayer, we begin to leave elephant tracks for others as well. We even give such prayers back to ourselves—songs we learn by day, then sing by night when we can no longer hear the music or see the words. I have many times been with a person suffering from dementia or Alzheimer's disease for whom words were to thoughts what square pegs are to round holes. One elderly woman, the mother of two loving daughters, broke my heart when during our fragmented visit she said randomly, "I'm the one that doesn't mother." And yet as soon as I began to speak the Lord's Prayer to close our time together, it was as though God were in heaven again, and all was right with her world. Word for word that prayer was prayed by this one who, in a way, had made her own firm imprints in the soil over many, many years. Now, in this moment when life was a pathless wood, she could still, when offered a hand to lead her, find her way to those familiar tracks, somehow hidden from pathology's insidious hunt, her own secret gift to herself of faith and order.

You, Lord, are all I have. You give me all I need. My life is in your hands. These words and their simple, boundless trust, have led many a sojourner, including this one, through thick and thin. The late J. T. Seamands first introduced me to this prayer at a Christian Ashram when I was a young teenager. He was paraphrasing Psalm 16:5 slightly as he made his way back from that elephant's footprint—I have never found this exact translation of the verse. When it comes to learning and teaching prayer, nothing about "imitate" is ever understood to mean "clone." To be formed in the prayers of others does not mean being pressed into their mold; God has no appetite for cookie-cutter Christians. To drink from an elephant's track is not to *become* an elephant but to benefit from its pilgrimage.

At the same time, God does not seem to care one way or another if our prayers have any sense of novelty about them. Earnestness, yes; deliberateness, certainly. But innovation? Wheel the soil across the lawn in your neighbor's old, beat-up wheelbarrow or carry it in your shiny, new bucket fresh off the sale rack and see if the bulbs you bury beneath that soil ever recognize the difference. If you want to pray, but are challenged as to how, begin with others' prayers. Take up a

Bible . . . "O Lord, you have searched me and known me . . .";
a hymnal . . . "Great is thy faithfulness . . ."; a prayerbook
. . . "Make me an instrument of thy peace . . ." Recall any
prayers you might have learned in childhood . . . "God, you
are kind and loving; kind and loving let us be . . ."; or from the
church gathered in worship "Be thou my vision, O Lord of
my heart . . ." When you have no words, and when you have
too many, borrow the most time-honored, time-honoring
prayer of all—the prayer of silence. "For God alone my soul
waits in silence . . ."

Pray these prayers once, twice, seventy times seven. "Forgive
us, Lord, as we forgive . . ." Pray them with emotion or pray
them with none, but pray them with intention, if not meaning
them completely, then with a *desire* to mean them. Better to
have the meaning and miss the experience than the reverse.
John Wesley, feeling at one point as though he was not worthy
to preach due to his own lack of faith, was deeply taken by the
counsel of a friend, Peter Bohler. Bohler told him, essentially,
to "preach faith till you have faith." If we were to apply the
same wisdom to prayer, we might say, "Don't worry if at first
you don't trust God or even yourself in your efforts to pray.
Pray as though and until you do, and then pray because you
have been given such trust."

*O God, who hast folded back the mantle of the night to clothe us in
the golden glory of the day, chase from our hearts all gloomy thoughts,
and make us glad with the brightness of hope, that we may effectively
aspire to unwon virtues, through Christ our Lord. Amen.*

This morning prayer found a place in my mother's spoken
prayers many times across the years of my childhood. As
prayers eventually will do among those who overhear them, it
made its way to an inner place in me where such prayers are
remembered beyond their hearing. Years later, I made my way
again and again to the place where that prayer had been kept,
first as a college student, then as a young pastor, then as a

parent myself, then as nobody in particular. Whoever embarks upon the journey of faith will along the way surely become acquainted with the night, but will at the same time grow in the assurance that the sun also rises. In fairer seasons, the first line of this prayer will have meant nothing more or less than waking from a good night's sleep to meet with readiness the new day's work. And then there are the other seasons, during which our approximations of sleep have brought more weariness than refreshment, and rising to the day's demands feels so hopeless as to require a strength greater than our own.

A few years ago I rediscovered among my things a small white prayer book, published in 1941, that had been given to me by parents whose teenager had been in the youth group I led one summer during my college years. Leafing through its pages, I savored the many beautiful prayers it held. As I turned a certain page, I drew my breath, recognizing from somewhere inside the words before me: "O God, who hast folded back the mantle of the night to clothe us in the golden glory of the day . . ." It was my mother's prayer. I read the prayer through to its end, where I found this inscription, printed in capital letters like a sign at the zoo: AN ANCIENT COLLECT, A.D. 590.

My mother, too, had found her way to an elephant's tracks. After all, prayer can be prayed only because prayer has been prayed. Those who teach us to pray have drawn from ancient prayers; the ancients drew from still older prayers; and those before them, from the primordial prayers of our very earliest stories of the faith, coming at last to one of the first: the prayer that originates not with the creature but the Creator: "Adam, Eve, where are you?" It is the original elephant's track, the *ur-*footprint, we might say, first imprinted in the mud by a Creator on a loving quest for the creature. It has since become very much our own prayer of seeking, drawn upon by creatures great and small, and from many a circumstance, as we embark on our own loving quest for our Creator. "God, where are you?" It is the prayer of absence seeking presence, aspiration seeking fulfillment, loneliness seeking belonging. It is the prayer of the one who believes as well as the one who wishes to believe, both of whom borrow others' words to express the very same human longing. That longing is nothing other than to meet the God who longs to meet us; to seek the God who never ceases seeking after us; to know and be known by the God who is finally all we really have, gives us all we will ever need, and in whose hands our lives are forever held.

Chapter 5

Something understood

Do not be like them, for your Father
knows what you need.
—Matthew 6:8

There may be nothing in this world more disheartening than the experience of being misunderstood. You can surely recall a time when being misunderstood resulted in deep if unintended hurt, maybe the rupture of a significant relationship, perhaps even the altering or derailing of your life's course. It is very likely that you tried everything you knew to correct the misunderstanding, and it is quite possible that by doing so you only made matters worse. The world is often generous enough to allow misunderstandings to be corrected and resolved. Often, but not always.

If being misunderstood can wound a life so deeply, nothing brings a more profound sense of validation and fulfillment than its opposite—the experience of being *understood*. To be seen for who we truly are, with our best intentions understood for what they really consist of—a menagerie of hurts and hopes, memories and fears, selfishness and generosity—is a human longing rarely surpassed by any other. Give me food, water, clothing, shelter, and livelihood. Grateful as I may be, I will still ask for one thing more: to be understood.

Jesus' Sermon on the Mount, found in Matthew 5–7, is many things. It is ethical treatise, instruction manual, and manifesto against religious manipulation. It is a primer on standing up for what is right, making amends with those who wrong you, practicing genuine piety, and living modestly. Beyond all these, the Sermon on the Mount is one thing more: an epistle of understanding. From the sermon's very first word, *makarioi*, "Blessed," Jesus speaks three chapters' worth of comfort, encouragement, and understanding. Whoever else he may be preaching to, he is addressing the misunderstood.

In the opening Beatitudes, Jesus stands against the enormous tide of popular opinion and prejudice, preaching words of blessing for those who, in every age including our own, are targets of misunderstanding and even hatred. To these who are the least regarded—the poor in spirit, the pure in heart, the mourners, the meek—he offers compassion, assurance, and understanding. In one grace-borne gesture he both validates their experience and promises the Lord's favor. The rest of us are left to overhear.

Beyond the Beatitudes, we could find much else in this remarkable sermon to illustrate its divine message of advocacy and understanding toward those short on both. One such touchstone comes with Jesus' instruction on prayer, specifically his introduction of the Lord's Prayer. We have already considered the Lord's Prayer in its context within Luke's Gospel. The same prayer, with slight differences, is found in the Sermon on the Mount (Matthew 6:7ff). In this instance, however, the prayer is offered not in response to a request to "teach us to pray" as in Luke, but as unsolicited instruction by Jesus. And in some of the most beautifully reassuring words in the Gospels, Jesus prefaces the prayer by saying, "Your Father knows what you need before you ask him" (6:8).

If I were of a doctrinaire frame of mind, I might take those words and use them as proof of the omniscience of God, or to reinforce a doctrine of predestination or predeterminism. However, if we give attention to the tone and message of the larger context for these words—the three-chapter sermon as a whole—we may recognize something else in this phrase, something less doctrinal and more pastoral: an assurance from Jesus that the God to whom we would pray knows us well, understands us through and through, and longs to provide for our every need. Later in his sermon, Jesus will repeat this assurance: "Indeed your heavenly Father knows that you need all these things" (6:32).

I believe these phrases have the character not of a life map but a canopy. When you pray, Jesus seems to be saying, bear in mind and take to heart this fundamental truth, and let it provide you with the deepest sense of trust and assurance as you approach your heavenly Father: God knows you, knows you well; knows your needs, your heart, your yearnings; knows your hopes and dreams, your blessings and bandages. God knows you the way you hope a lifelong friend will eventually come to know you. Understand this, Jesus seems to say: prayer is, before and after all else, understanding that you are understood.

The English poet George Herbert once wrote a four-stanza poem titled "Prayer." Situated within a larger work called *The Temple*, "Prayer" presents an uninterrupted sequence of metaphors, some twenty-seven in all, each representing prayer. The poem reads like a busy wren building, twig by twig, the nest he anticipates will be home to him and his yet-to-be-discovered mate. "Reversed thunder," "Engine against the Almightie," "The soul in paraphrase." Image after image fills out the nature of that intricate and many-splendored encounter with God we know as prayer. "Exalted manna," "Heaven in ordinarie, earth well dressed." The linkage of twigs is taking the form of a hollowed-out vessel. "Heart in pilgrimage," "a kind of tune." At the final phrase of the poem's final verse, the female wren has arrived on the scene, cushioning the nest of twigs with shreds and bits of leaves, moss, grass, and wool—things found in the soft underbelly of our lives. The two birds' work is now complete, and they settle into their soft and sturdy home, a final pair of words within a nest of words: "Something understood."

With these two closing words of the poem, Herbert provides us with a sublime description of the situated end of a prayer that has arrived roundabout at some insight, assurance, or acceptance. Prayer has done its long and labored work, struggling, wrenching, raising its fist; and also feasting, singing, floating as a feather on the wind. With jutting twigs and waxen leaves, it has fashioned a home, structured and warm, for the home-seeking heart: something has been understood.

Right away, new questions are born. What is understood? By whom? Is prayer God understanding us, or us understanding God? And why is only *something* understood—why not *all*? Herbert's poem, doing what poetry does for a living, leaves these matters suspended in a rich ambiguity. The reader—in this case, you—is left to raise the question of what the experience of prayer affords, that is, of what is finally understood.

In prayer, do you understand God more clearly, or sense more clearly God's understanding of you? Does the lamp raised in the time of silence and sighing, asking and *alleluia* illumine the divine, or your own heart, or in some measure both? And if not everything comes clear in prayer; if the raised lantern not only sheds light but also creates new shadows, is the acceptance of the shadows part of the understanding? In other words, is the allowance of what we cannot know a knowing all its own? And what about the world—what do we see differently in holding the world before God in prayer? How do we now regard the war-ravaged country for which we have interceded, the person in the next car over, the friend in the hospital, the family member from whom we have been estranged?

Further, how does society come to understand those of its number who pray, who instead of shouting choose instead to whisper? "Pray in secret," Jesus counsels his listeners elsewhere in this sermon, warning against showing off our religion. What do we say to the world by not saying anything but rather quietly finding our way to the sanctuary or prayer room to repair the world from the margins? Jesus says earlier in this sermon that when others see our good works—not placed on display for an admiring public, but practiced discreetly for their own inherent goodness—they will glorify God. Prayer begetting prayer.

Maybe with the placement of "something understood" at the very end of a freewheeling, far-ranging succession of metaphors, Herbert was suggesting that the experience of prayer seldom involves instantly hearing a direct word of guidance or grace, as though through a megaphone. We come to insight or assurance, rather, by means more akin to what in Hebrew is known as a *bat kol*, the daughter of a voice. For it is often by indirection that we arrive at a place of direction. It was Paul Tillich who wrote that "here and there in the world and now and then in ourselves is a New Creation." A little something here, another something there. Some insight now, more then. The life of prayer is constructed of just such reported glimpses—a twig, a blade of grass, a clump of moss; hearsay fashioned into home.

And home, as we know, is the name given to people and places where understanding is the norm. It is the place where they more or less read our shorthand, and we theirs; where on a good day hopes and dreams and needs are largely known before they are ever voiced. "Your Father knows what you need before you ask." Home is the nest in which we come to settle wherever we are, whoever we are with or away from, and in the midst of whatever work we happen to be doing when we discover that God loves us in such an encompassing way, and possesses such an unfathomable sense for our well-being, and for the world's. Apprehended by this one truth, this one promise, this one assurance, words come to their end. But we give them up freely, for in their place has settled something far better; in their place is something understood.

> Prayer the Churches banquet, Angels age,
> Gods breath in man returning to his birth,
> The soul in paraphrase, heart in pilgrimage,
> The Christian plummet sounding heav'n and earth:
> Engine against th' Almightie, sinners towre,
> Reversed thunder, Christ-side-piercing spear,
> The six-daies world transposing in an houre,
> A kind of tune, which all things heare and fear;
> Softnesse, and peace, and joy, and love, and blisse,
> Exalted Manna, gladnesse of the best,
> Heaven in ordinaire, man well drest,
> The milkie way, the bird of Paradise,
> Church-bels beyond the starres heard, the souls bloud,
> The land of spices; something understood.

George Herbert, from *The Temple*

part
two

Habits of the heart

The work of seeing is done.

Now practice heart-work. . . .

Rainer Maria Rilke

Chapter 6

The broth of false and true

My heart is steadfast, O God, my heart is steadfast.
Psalm 57:7

The heart is deceitful above all things.
Jeremiah 17:9 KJV

We sometimes speak of the heart as the clearinghouse where mind and body, emotions and will, memory and hope all merge. It is as though these are literally carried in the blood that from every corner and reach of our natural being courses into the middle of our chest and through the unresting organ stationed there. The chambers that make up the physical heart go by names surely inspired as much by philosophy as anatomy: atrium and ventricle. "Atrium" means open to the sky, and we have already explored the idea of our hearts opening like a book before God. "Ventricle" means empty belly; and hunger, whether in the stomach or the heart, is a force to be reckoned with. In one sense, the heart vaults upward toward the sky, all our best intentions in tow; in another, it rummages and roots deep in the gut, unearthing all manner of instincts, appetites, and fears as it forages for its supper in the hungering dark.

If prayer is something the Spirit helps us to do, something others have done before us to our benefit; if prayer promises to be so ineffable an experience of understanding and being understood, then considering the heart's anatomy helps us see why the practice of being in God's presence elicits such mixed response. An informal poll on whether we believe in the value of prayer, the power of prayer, the importance of a vital relationship with God would have us all lifting our hands with a certain umbilical ease, as though we had been asked if we favored oxygen. The poll completed, we are likely to pick up our gnawed pencil and resume the laundry list of daily doubts and fears. Mystery of mysteries, the human heart is attuned both to upward calling and downward foraging, to things expansive and things meager. At the twinkling of an eye we all behave unrecognizably, experience feelings completely unrehearsed, or turn from a chosen way to one long since rejected, any one of these leading in either favorable or unfavorable directions. When pivoting toward goodness or away, the heart is nimble as an airborne swallow.

The Bible offers a perspective on the heart that only confirms this bivocational nature. We read in its pages that the heart is the most deceitful thing in all the world, and also that it can be steadfast as the North Star. Further complicating this contradictory picture is that both assessments can apply to one and the same heart. Simon Peter is the poster child of interruptible fidelity. At Caesarea Philippi he offers Jesus and those around a glowing witness: "You are the Messiah, the Son of the living God" (Matthew 16:16). Then, having just pronounced Jesus the anointed of God, he turns around and challenges him (16:22). Some time later, just before Jesus is arrested, Peter pledges his loyalty, even if it means prison—or death

(Luke 22:33). Later that night, after Jesus' arrest, Peter, following at a safe distance, warms himself beside a makeshift fire while Jesus is being bullied nearby. But at least he is *there*, more than can be said of the other disciples. The problem with warming yourself by the fire, of course, is that it is an inherently social activity. Standing there in the fire's glow, he is recognized by a servant-girl as one of Jesus' followers. The "Rock" becomes defensive. "Woman, I do not know him," he insists, inverting the earlier meaning of "glowing witness." He will offer this denial twice again over the next couple of hours. Not until Jesus looks in his direction does Peter understand what he has done, and the realization cuts like a knife (Luke 22:54-62). The Greek term used to describe his reaction is not employed again for any other purpose in any of the four Gospels, having been reserved for this tragic moment and its tragic figure alone: He wept *bitterly*.

It is clear that when we take up the subject of the human heart, we hold in our hands an artistic work that falls into the category of mixed media. Frederick Buechner was speaking to this blended classification when he wrote that "nothing human's not a broth of false and true." One moment we prove ourselves trustworthy and devoted; the next, we demonstrate the capacity to be deceptive and detached. One season we experience the practices of the faith as life-giving; the next, they are as much use to us as two tails to a dog. In one setting we may possess a heightened sense of spiritual awareness; change the scenery, and gross motor skills take over, leaving us to wonder if the earlier experience of transcendence was just the coffee.

Which are our true colors, deception or devotion? I think the Bible would answer most unhelpfully that *both* are, that decent people sometimes do wrong and hurtful things, and that, likewise, mean and selfish people are remarkably capable of decency and even kindness. We are sinful creatures, "prone to wander, Lord, I feel it . . ." *and* we are made in the image of

God. We are stuck in the gripping birdlime of deadness, as Augustine once so vividly put it, *and* we are eligible to be raised up to life and freedom by the grace of Jesus Christ through the power of the Holy Spirit. The physical heart represents with fluid fidelity the lifelong quandary of this pushmi-pullyu existence.

Some years ago I participated in the Dallas marathon, always held in early December when temperatures tend to be mild. On this December morning the temperatures *were* mild—to a Canadian: 20 degrees Farenheit at the beginning of the race. The starting gun sounded, and off we went, thousands of sniffling, teeth-chattering, rosy-cheeked runners winding our way north from City Hall through uptown neighborhood streets. The field ran the gamut from professionals to amateurs like me, but it is safe to say we all shared at least one basic understanding: the importance of hydration. Even in cold weather, the body under exertion must replenish its water resources frequently to avoid injury and sustain performance. During a long race such as a marathon, water stations are lifelines.

The name "water station" is something of a misnomer. These are often water *and sports drink* stations, at which volunteers holding out cups to passing runners continuously shout out the contents of their paper cups, whether water or a sports drink. For runners looking specifically for one or the other, this practice saves time and avoids confusion.

The first water station in the marathon that morning, about three miles into the race, was a true water station—offering only water. The volunteers held the small paper cups in their outstretched hands as they shouted over and over the standard line: "Water! . . . Water! . . . Water!" Runners hardly slowed their pace as they snatched the cups and continued running, sloshing water as they went. From the very first messy hand-offs came an outcome the race planners never would have anticipated: spilled water on frozen pavement. Normally, a little water on the street would be of no concern, but in these temperatures the wet pavement around the water station turned icy in a hurry. As approaching runners discovered this treacherous footing, they instinctively shouted a word of caution to runners behind them to stay clear of the area: "Ice! . . . Ice! . . . Ice!" As I drew near the water station, I heard two words being shouted simultaneously by different people—one an invitation, the other a warning: "Water! *Ice!* Water! *Ice!*" I felt like Alice in Wonderland. Canadian Wonderland.

As we approach the subject of the habits of the heart, we will do well to think of the heart as a water station on a really frigid race day, and then to listen for these overlapping shouts of invitation and warning, recognizing the intimate proximity between devotion and deception. The distance between the two is the variance between water and ice—a degree or two up or down, and one becomes the other. It is the difference between a single word spoken or withheld, the stroke of this key rather than the next one over, a passing glance and one that lingers a second or two longer. Choosing almost true over true is often as slight a thing as stepping over a crack in the sidewalk. We are diminished by the choice, but not noticeably. Encouraged by our apparent resilience, we repeat the behavior the next time, and are diminished only a little more, and again, until one day we have grown sufficiently small for the crack in the sidewalk to swallow us whole.

The other choice, for true over almost true, is one to which we are born, and for which others prepare and pray over us from the waters of the womb to the waters of our baptism and well beyond. It is the way of responsibility accepted if not always eagerly chosen, which is to say, the way of grace. Whether we are guided by what is true enthusiastically or under obligation matters less than the decision to follow that guidance. With every such decision, witness is made to one another and the watching world of God's goodness to redeem. The heart has opened skyward like the pages of a book. And the sky, as we have seen, has gifts to offer—nightly wonders yielding daily bread.

Chapter 7

After passion

And those who belong to Christ Jesus have crucified the
flesh with its passions and desires.
Galatians 5:24

What's your passion? You've got to follow your passion. I feel really passionate about this. It's clear to me where your passion lies. These are some of the ways we commonly speak about our sense of purpose, direction, and calling in life. In contemporary wisdom, passion is the password for identifying what matters most, means the most, promises the most personal and vocational fulfillment. Passion is the password, and everyone is after it. Movies, magazines, and motivational speakers champion the idea, presenting one scenario after another of those whose lives have been transformed by the discovery of their inner passion. If we want to know which sign to follow, call to answer, road to travel, gift or talent or interest to cultivate, we are led to believe we need only answer one simple question, "What is my passion?"

Popular music, energy drinks, adventure tours, pharmaceutical aids, automotive ads, and the general fixation in our society on living with sustained intensity further fuel the pursuit of passion. Life is somehow thought to be better if lived exponentially rather than simply lived. We have trained our appetites away from the vegetables we're slicing to the glint on the edge of the cutting knife, indifferent to the fact that only the former is edible.

Among my concerns regarding these impassioned ways we have been taught to think and converse about life and vocation, this one stands out: they subvert our normative theological understanding of faith and human emotion. In Scripture and the Christian tradition, "passion" is a word generally used to describe feelings and impulses that manipulate, mislead, and destroy. Passions separate us from God and one another by turning us in on ourselves, then outward upon others in controlling rather than developing ways. When understood in this context, the first string of questions that passion raises, in one form or another, is *What is my need, my hunger, my itch, and how can I satisfy it?* Only then, if at all, does it ask, *What is the world's need, and how can I help meet it?* While this is certainly not always the case, "passion" language easily slides into a grammar that begins the conversation with *my* call and claim upon God and the world, whereas Christian language begins by speaking of *God's* call and claim upon *us* and the world. For people of faith, the difference is whether we will speak in terms of self-fulfillment or self-giving. What we know on good authority is that the latter results in what the former seeks.

When the late Christopher Reeve, who suffered severe paralysis following a horse-riding accident in 1995, was asked what was the most difficult lesson he had learned from his experience, he said, "I'm very clear about it. I know I have to give when sometimes I really want to take." He was referring specifically to his experience as a human being with extreme disabilities and a tremendous number of dependencies, but he could just as well have been referring to his experience as a human being—*period*. His most difficult lesson happens to be anyone's most difficult lesson: we have to give when sometimes we really want to take. The truth, of course, is that not only is giving in such instances the right thing to do, the practice of healthy self-denial also shapes us into those persons of faith we have vowed at our baptism to allow God to make of us.

The Christian life involves slowly and patiently submitting to the slow and patient work of the Holy Spirit to form us in dispositions and behaviors of loving God through serving others. Unlike myself in the sentence you just read, Paul the apostle minces no words on this subject in his letter to the Galatians, pronouncing rather emphatically that we have "crucified the flesh with its passions and desires." Just earlier, he identifies those dispositions and behaviors that sprout up in the very place where inordinate passions and desires have been felled. He calls them "the fruit of the Spirit," and then he calls them by name: love, joy, peace, patience, kindness, generosity, faithfulness, gentleness, and self-control (Galatians 5:22). The ancient wisdom applies to us no less than to the young Galatian church: through self-absorption, fulfillment evaporates like mist in the sunlight; through self-giving, fulfillment flourishes beneath those same rays like a garden, yielding its treasures of blossom, fragrance, and fruit beyond what we could ever enjoy alone.

What the Bible seems most concerned about is not whether there is energy and emotion around a certain task or undertaking but the source and direction for that energy and emotion—whether that source is within or beyond us. To put it another way, imagine that in front of every heart rests an altar with room enough to kneel on either side. To kneel toward the heart and away from God is to regard personal emotions and feelings as the guide for right behaviors and choices. We are saying, effectively, I will follow my heart, for whatever my heart says must be true. To kneel away from the heart and toward God expresses trust in the God who knit us together in our mother's womb, and whose concern is for me, to be sure, but also and equally for the rest of the world, knit together by those same hands. It says, I choose to follow God and let my feelings follow suit. In the former posture, we come to occupy an expansive mountain lodge, but with boarded-up windows; in the latter, a simple room, but with the grandest of views.

I enjoy cycling outdoors, and have occasionally dropped in on an indoor spin class as well. I once attended such a class at the fitness center near my office. The equipment was state-of-the-art, with digital read-out screens on each bicycle that monitored pace, distance, elapsed time, and so forth. The screen also featured a small heart icon at the bottom, which I supposed was for the purpose of displaying heart-rate readings. In the course of the hour, a number appeared on my screen next to the heart icon. I was intrigued—the handlebars must be taking the reading from my hands. Then the number on the screen began to climb, and by the end of the hour my exercising heart rate was much higher than normal. I decided I had put in quite an impressive workout. Curious, I lingered after class to ask the instructor what he thought my ideal exercising heart rate should be. When he told me, I explained that the number on the monitor had been a lot higher. He asked to have a look at my chest strap unit. "What chest strap unit?" I asked. He explained that the monitors take their information from a wireless unit positioned on the rider's chest. When I told him I didn't have one, he chuckled and said, "Your bike was probably reading the output from the person on the bike next to you—it happens all the time."

When we kneel toward the heart rather than away, the results can be very impressive, and wildly deceiving. The sentiments of the heart, when put in charge, often lead us in all sorts of colorful but also potentially hurtful directions. In a different mood, the heart can also be fickle as a Friday night, leading us on with some newfound endeavor, then dropping the interest just as quickly. If the popular phrase, "What's your passion?" has a counterpart, it may be "My heart's not in it." Why did you stop teaching the class? My heart's not in it. Why did you give up working at the shelter? My heart was no longer in it. I picture a support group for those whose heart is now out of whatever it was once in. Going around the circle, there is a surgeon who left the operating room during a delicate brain surgery, a pastor who failed to show up for a funeral, a firefighter who walked away from a blazing apartment building, and a bus driver who left the crowded bus idling between two bus stops—all because their hearts were no longer in what they were doing. Meetings of the "My-Heart-Is-No-Longer-In-It" support group are helpful for those who participate, but attendance tends to be spotty.

Let me be clear that a critique of the notion of passion as a password to personal fulfillment does not diminish the primacy of enthusiasm, excitement, or emotion in human experience. Enthusiasm (the word means "God within") fills the pages of Scripture like wine a chalice—to the brim and even over. As for excitement, a phrase used repeatedly in the New Testament is "the power of the Holy Spirit." Most would agree that the Greek word for this power, *dunamis*, as in "dynamite," fairly promises a robust experience for those in its proximity.

Finally, emotion is at the heart of human experience, including the human experience of God. To be loved and to love are the cornerstones of faith, and love, of course, has a fundamentally emotional aspect. Further, to be human is to be alive to an unspeakably intricate kaleidoscope of sense, emotion, and intuition in their infinite combinations. We can befriend these feelings and intuitions, enjoy and trust and even honor them. But friends do not good monarchs make. Placing our feelings on a throne can lead to tyrannies ranging far beyond the boundaries of our own skin. As we noted a chapter earlier, there is refreshment to be drawn from the heart, but hazards are always nearby.

After passion has been set aside as a primary source of insight and direction, and we have determined that feelings are not altogether reliable field guides, what is to lead us to vocation and fulfillment? If my own levels of enthusiasm and excitement are not an accurate gauge of the importance and worth of a certain pursuit, then what will serve as that gauge? Once again, Paul provides us with a key. Following his pointed words to the Galatians about crucifying the flesh with its passions and desires, he writes, "If we live by the Spirit, let us also be guided by the Spirit" (Galatians 5:25). The Holy Spirit is understood and experienced by Paul as the means by which the magnificent muddle of the human heart can be guided and grown into a place of order and beauty. If the heart is a garden, the Spirit waits to be its wise and patient gardener. I say *waits* only because the garden's gate opens from the inside.

Chapter 8

The listening heart

. . . the Advocate, the Holy Spirit, whom the Father will send in my name, will teach you everything, and remind you of all that I have said to you.
John 14:26

Where would we be without prepositions? I am speaking of those little words that appear around, before, and after the big words to arrange everything just so. A preposition literally *pre*-positions what follows it, setting up whatever is going to be said in this way or that. You might say that prepositions are the trip planners of the sentence, determining whether, when we come to the fork in the road, we will go left or right. And the way chosen makes all the difference. Do we laugh *at* someone or *with* someone? Fall *from* grace or *with* grace? Will the trip to Grandmother's house take us *over* the river and *through* the woods, or *along* the river and *around* the woods? The way I see it, any old cow can jump *under* the moon; it takes a real heifer to jump *over* it.

Now for the preposition that concerns us at the moment. We have two words that need to be steered a certain way: "listening" and "heart." What direction will they take? What will be their relationship? It seems two options are available to us:

listening *to* the heart and listening *with* the heart. Borrowing the altar image from the previous chapter, to face inward as we kneel is to choose a disposition of listening *to* the heart, understanding our own feelings and emotions as the guide for our decisions and actions. On the other hand, to face outward as we kneel suggests listening *with* the heart, understanding God to be the one who provides guidance for our lives by means of the Holy Spirit. When we kneel in this direction, feelings and emotions are not denied but join us at the altar to seek a wider view. The Christian life is one of choosing more and more to seek the Holy Spirit's guidance as indicated by a specific preposition: listening *with* the heart. The hope is for time and use to wear the altar smooth on the side that faces God.

How does the Holy Spirit give guidance through our kneeling toward God and listening with the heart? In John's narrative of Jesus' parting words to his disciples, sometimes called the "farewell discourse," we are given a name, and with it, an insight. For our purposes, the name Jesus gives the Holy Spirit is as instructive as what he says the Spirit will do. He calls the Holy Spirit "Advocate" (in Greek, *Parakleo*). Advocate and *Parakleo* have identical root meanings. *Ad* and *para* both mean "toward." *Vocate* and *kleo* suggest the word "call" in the sense of "to call" or "to be called." The Advocate is one who calls toward, or is called toward.

It is unclear whether the tense implied in this word is active or passive; that is, has Jesus given the Holy Spirit the name "One Who Calls Toward" or "One Who Is Called Toward"? The question may seem esoteric—interesting to only the most serious word buffs—but it has important theological implications regarding the place of the Holy Spirit in our lives. Is the role of the Holy Spirit to summon us to faithful living, or to be summoned by us for comfort, assurance, instruction, and remembrance? Does God call upon *us*, or do we call upon God? The meaning of the name as Jesus uses it is not precise—

it has a background as both an active word (calls toward) and a passive word (is called toward).

This may, however, be an instance in which the ambiguity of a word lends accuracy rather than vagueness. Think of the relationship of parents and their children. Do the parents call the child toward love, learning, discipline, and discovery? Or are the parents called toward the child for comfort, security, food, clothing, and shelter? We know, of course, that both are true: parents call toward and are called toward; likewise their children, in inverse relationship, call and are called. When lovers meet in mutual intimacy, each summons the other, and is, in the same encounter, summoned. Friends sharing the miracle of conversation first accept the listening ear of the other, then offer it in return in what is normally an unconscious rhythm of giving and receiving. When, with time, that reciprocity becomes second nature rather than self-conscious, the friendship has reached a satisfying maturity.

The mystery of our lives is that asking and being asked are woven together as the warp and weft of a tapestry. Religion, as I have noted in other writings, means *to tie together again.* To be religious is not so much a matter of performing certain rituals as it is the simultaneous overtures of our calling on God to see the rended world to wholeness, and God's calling on us for the same. In the process of fulfilling that shared yearning, we are both shepherd and shepherded. God is here for us, providing love and vision for our part in the task, and we are here for God as instruments in that work. The word Paul chooses to describe the arrangement is *sunergia,* or "synergy" (2 Corinthians 6:1). The German word for worship is also helpful here. *Goddesdienst,* which translates to mean "the service of God," succinctly suggests that we gather in worship both to serve God *and* to be served by God.

In one and the same gesture we seek the Holy Spirit and are sought by the Holy Spirit. While hearing the call, "Whom shall I send?" we are already speaking a response, "Here I am; send me." And while we pray, "O God, come to my assistance," God has already spoken the reply, "I am with you always." Ann and Barry Ulanov had it right when they wrote, together, that the spiritual is a realm not of sequence but simultaneity.

The Advocate, then, calls us toward God even while being called toward us. What this suggests is that guidance of the individual by the Holy Spirit and answering the Holy Spirit's greater call go hand in hand. For in putting our hand in God's hand, and following God's leading, we may begin to discern a more particular direction for our lives. It is no coincidence that the word *obey* derives from the Latin "to hear." To yield to God's larger purposes is to begin to have the ear opened to God's specific guidance for our own lives. Earlier in John 14, Jesus makes a connection between following God and experiencing God's guidance in this very way, clearly linking obedience with revelation: "They who have my commandments and *keep them* are those who love me . . . and I will love them and *reveal myself to them*" (John 14:21, italics mine).

The commandments of which Jesus is speaking are elsewhere in John and the New Testament summed up in a single teaching: to love one another (e.g., John 13:34-35; Romans 13:8-10). Love one another, and you will see Jesus revealed. Put another way, raise a lantern in your window to light the way of the wayfaring stranger and that light will come to reveal the Christ in your very midst, both welcomed and welcoming.

When I was younger, I asked in many different ways for God to guide my life, direct my path, order my steps. I harbored the sense that God had a specific plan for me, and if I were to listen closely, I would discern just what that plan was to be. "Show me your will, O God," was my prayer. I continue to this day to pray that prayer, but one thing has changed. In college, when I first began seriously seeking God's purpose for my life, I discovered that revelation had more of the look and feel of a relationship than a road map. Its purpose appeared to be coaching rather than corralling. Over time, my questions about guidance and direction began to evolve from "Where shall I go?" to "*How* shall I go there?" From "What should I do with my life?" to "Whatever the particular course I take, how can I live that life in such a way that God is at its center?" I vividly recall how in my senior year of college I came upon a prayer in the letter to the Colossians that spoke about God's will not as a specific set of coordinates but as a *manner* of living, a *way* of *being* with God in the world: "We have not ceased praying for you and asking that you may be filled with the knowledge of *God's will* in all spiritual wisdom and understanding, so that you may *lead lives worthy of the Lord*, fully pleasing to him, as you *bear fruit in every good work* and as you grow *in the knowledge of God*" (Colossians 1:9-11, italics mine). It seemed increasingly clear that the will of God for my life was to be in relationship with Christ, allowing the vocational particulars of what, where, and when to emerge in the process.

Very soon other familiar passages began to shed a similar light: God "has told you, O mortal, what is good; and what does the LORD require of you but to do justice, and to love kindness, and walk modestly with your God" (Micah 6:8; translation mine). "Do not be conformed to this world, but be transformed by the renewing of your minds, so that you may discern what is the will of God—what is good and acceptable and perfect" (Romans 12:2). "Thy word is a lamp unto my feet, and a light unto my path" (Psalm 119:105 KJV).

What does God want for your life? That you be a butcher, a baker, or a candlestick maker? That you go to school? Start to work? That you retire now, or work another five years? That you give $500 to the church, or $5,000, or $50,000? That you accept a job transfer and move your family, or decline it and stay where you are? I am not suggesting there are no specific answers to these questions; only that what interests God more than particular roles or choices is that we lead lives that are worthy, pleasing, and fruit-bearing; that we do justice, love kindness, and walk modestly with God as our companion and guide; that we be transformed over time by the renewal of our minds; that we allow God's teachings so fully into the journey of our lives that they become a source of illumination not only to our *heads* but also to our *feet*.

Over time what God wants and what we want begin to merge into the same will and purpose: the world made whole, ourselves included. Listening *with* the heart has begun to encompass listening *to* the heart, leaving both prepositions to pack up and seek employment elsewhere. What remains is simply the listening heart, one that hears God and its own yearnings in one and the same whisper. The altar before the heart is now as obsolete as the prepositions that had divided its purpose. The *obedient* heart, which is to say, the *listening* heart, has itself become the altar; its offering, our living devotion.

Chapter 9

Whispering in church

*O sing to the L*ORD *a new song;*
*sing to the L*ORD*, all the earth.*
Psalm 96:1

When our listening hearts are attuned to the divine whisper, what we are bound to hear first and foremost is a human voice. No matter how high in the mountains we have traveled to escape "the madding crowd" in order to listen for God, or how remote our retreat cabin once we arrive; no matter how long we stay in that isolation, or how deep our self-imposed silence while we are there, when the time comes to receive a message about God's love for us being lived out through us in particular ways, the words we hear whispered in our ear will undoubtedly bear the accent of someone we know.

It may be the fourth-grade Sunday school teacher who had us memorize Psalm 23, and in whose voice we still hear it spoken. It may be a father or a mother who read us nursery rhymes when we were children or helped us cobble together our bedtime prayers. It may be the author of a certain book whose voice, though we have never actually heard it, is as audible to us as if they had been reading aloud from a chair across the room. It may be a grandmother, a pastor, a schoolteacher; a friend, a neighbor, a choir director. But it will be a voice with skin. When we go away by ourselves to an isolated place in order to hear from God, we should bring along extra linens for the guests that are sure to drop in on the conversation.

If we think the voice we hear on such occasions is the voice of God it is probably because we have an active imagination, and also because, in a very real sense, it *is* the voice of God. I never cease to be amazed how often the meat and bread of God's communications are carried on a raven's wing rather than an angel's (1 Kings 17:1-7). Never one to be fancy when the ordinary will do, God seems to budget for messengers like the owner of a rag and bone shop: if there is a shortage of what you are looking for, lower your standards until you arrive at plenty. At least Elijah got ravens; Balaam got a jackass. The spies on Jericho got a harlot. Ruth got a man who could have been her father. For Noah, it was a dove, more commonly referred to as a street pigeon. Jonah got an insider's view of a big fish. Abraham, a ram. The world got a peasant born in a stable who spent his first few nights sleeping in a feed trough, and probably his first few weeks smelling like one.

I don't know if what we are discussing here is God's will or God's wit, so close are the two in outward appearance. Placing humans in the role of shouldering the weighty responsibility and unspeakable privilege of being the bearers of God's presence and purpose is, when we consider the material, quite a mixed proposition. Let's be honest—we are about as lumbering as we are lithe, swans gliding gracefully on water but waddling worrisomely on land. We mix our metaphors, forget the shopping list, prod the elevator button, accelerate to stop lights, sleep under blankets in summer.

If only that were all. We lie to one another, steal from one another, say one thing and do another, hurt those we love the most, enthrall ourselves with those we've never met. We lose our tempers, kick the dog, drink ourselves silly, grow old alone.

We go to war on pretense, raze whole rain forests for an inch or two of soil, buy mufflers costing more because they muffle less, and eat and run, but hate to. We linger at mirrors, though with shifting eyes, pronounce casually that something is awesome, and pay good money to tour nature's wonders, but only briefly—we're meeting friends for dinner.

Some days we are not much more than a blend of the court jester and the rodeo clown. Nonetheless, for some reason we have been created and commissioned to invite one another into relationship with the God of both history and—thank goodness—hope. And so we go about that task, even if haphazardly or unawares. When we sing "Alleluia!" it is not God we are addressing but the person next to us. The word means "Praise the Lord!" and is our way of schooling one another in how to behave in a moment of weariness or wonder. The Psalms, what we often call the Bible's prayer book—are filled with such lateral "alleluias." In fact, if we were doing a pie chart of that particular collection of prayers to identify when they talk to God and when to people, we would end up with a generous slice of the pie served up to *us* rather than God: "Sing to the LORD a new song . . ."; "This is the day that the LORD has made . . ."; and "I was glad when they said to me, 'Let us go to the house of the LORD!'" When we read aloud Psalm 23, we notice right away that we are praying part of the time, and giving testimony the rest: "The LORD is my shepherd . . . for you are with me . . . ; You prepare a table before me . . . ; and I shall dwell in the house of the LORD . . ." We may feel like saying, *Make up your mind—pray or preach!* Any psalmist worth their salt would surely answer, *To pray is to preach. To worship God is to show you how.* For there is no devotion that is not also testimony, and every act of prayer is a paving stone set along a path others soon enough will walk.

We have been seeking to answer the question of how the listening heart hears the whispered will of God, experiences

God as real, knows the purposes of God for our lives. The discussion so far has come just shy of an answer. It is as though we were twisting the stem of an apple in the school cafeteria, every twist a letter . . . A . . . B . . . C . . . waiting for the twist that breaks the stem and tells us the first letter of the name of the girl, the boy with whom we are destined to find puppy love—at least for that week. It is lunch in the service of love. In our case, it is twist . . . the heart is a broth . . . twist . . . passion is a dubious guide . . . twist . . . obedience places us closer to hearing . . .

The twist that finally severs the stem from the apple is both obvious and elusive, whether you are a kid in school or a grown-up in the world; that is, that lunch in the service of love has less to do with the boy in khakis across the room, or the girl in pigtails, than the mom or dad back home who put the apple in our lunch to begin with. Love is not the incantation around the stem, and where it will lead us; love is the apple, and where it has come from. This may seem backward, but I believe God's will is about source more than direction. If I know from whom I have come, and the community that has both called me to the font and sent me from it, then these sources become the basis for my understanding of where I am to go and who I am to be. The severed stem we hold between our fingers points from apple to tree, then back again.

Up to now, the Lord's Prayer has been approached in this book, but never yet entered into, as though we have been peering through the windows of a farm house as we wait for the farmer to return from the fields to welcome us in. Our host has arrived; the Lord's Prayer is before us. Actually, it is the *praying* of the Lord's Prayer I would invite us to overhear. One of the holiest moments in a worship hour occurs in what is essentially the only time whispering in church is ever encouraged. We lower our heads or raise them, clasp our hands together or take a hand nearby. A hush fills the room, and no single voice is any longer heard, but all are heard together as we begin to pray in unison, "Our Father, who art in heaven . . ."

As we pray, we behave very much like the psalms—overhearing one another as much as talking directly to God. And what we overhear is something that is true when whispered in a way it would not be if shouted; that is, that the community is bigger than we are. If you get a frog in your throat, forget for a moment the order of the words, or get tickled or distracted and fall silent, the church goes right on praying for you, and in spite of you, never pausing, never slowing, murmuring those sacred words right through to the "Amen." Besides being the best illustration you will ever see of compliance with the Bible's injunction to pray without ceasing, in that act of advancing the prayer without diversion or delay the worshiping community enacts its own congregational ethic. It demonstrates a certain holy indifference that, with regard to both the individual and the body as a whole, cares not a whit about the whims of either but harbors the utmost concern for the well-being of both.

In what is at once the most obvious and the least noticed feature of the Lord's Prayer, the gathered community will never once use the words "I" or "me" in praying it. In no sense whatsoever is this a solitary prayer; on the contrary, it is the most populated prayer in the Good Book, drawing into its tether the expanse of heaven, the realm of earth, people—including the adverse variety—and the Evil One. Teach *us* to pray, was the petition the disciples posed. And Jesus took them at their word—*that* word. The prayer he taught them was not for *me*, it was for *us* in the widest sense. This prayer will not fit in our pockets or purses any more than would the Milky Way. Its realm is God and the globe, and ours is the good fortune of belonging to both, from which we ask in this very prayer to be granted, among other things, the apple in our lunch, otherwise referred to as daily bread.

If there were only one thing the listening heart could know regarding God's will for the life of the person it represents, then that one thing would be a truth that week after week is whispered in church in the form of a prayer that is not so much prayed as enacted. It is the truth that the experience of the Christian community's holy indifference to my heart's whims, coupled with an utmost concern for its well-being, is one of the greatest gifts we will ever receive in life. Slow—even sluggish—in its wending work, this simultaneous caring and not caring is of such power as to redeem the broth of false and true that we are, cultivate in us the fruit of the Spirit, and guide us by means of that gardening Advocate in the way that leads to life abundant. It is in this prayer's enactment, first in worship, then beyond, that *thy will be done* comes to be fulfilled as far and wide as the whole of earth, and as near and narrow as that swath of it that is the listening heart.

Chapter 10

The power of our reluctance

A man had two sons; he went to the first and said,
"Son, go and work in the vineyard today." He answered,
"I will not"; but later he changed his mind and went.
The father went to the second and said the same;
and he answered, "I go, sir"; but he did not go.
Which of the two did the will of his father?
Matthew 21:28-31a

I have been around long enough to know that we would pay a lot of money for a car that will go wherever we please before accepting for free one that will only take us where we ought to go. Telling someone what is right to do and expecting them to do it agreeably in every instance is like expecting a cat to enjoy playing dress-up with a preschooler. The autonomous will has a will of its own, and human behavior maintains its reputation for mystery. Paul was right as rain when he wrote, "For I do not do the good I want, but the evil I do not want is what I do . . . when I want to do what is good, evil lies close at hand" (Romans 7:19, 21). It has been observed that when God builds a church, the devil builds a chapel. I have come to understand that churches and chapels are built not only on city streets and country lanes but also upon the real estate known as the human heart.

I would say that such ambivalence on our part is a force to be reckoned with, but it would be more accurate to say it is *two* forces to be reckoned with. We would not be resistant to following God if some alternative were not presenting itself as equally attractive. Nor does the alternative normally involve something as idle as kicking a pebble down the sidewalk. Important things keep us from the ways of God. "First let me go and bury my father," one would-be follower of Jesus requested, with what we would surely agree was real legitimacy. "Let me first say farewell to those at my home," implored another (Luke 9:59ff). Ambivalence arises not from the dilemma of a poor choice over against a better choice, but a good choice right up next to the best choice.

Moses is regarded as the greatest prophet in the Bible, yet the record of his reluctance when called by God to the prophet's work extends for chapters on end. Isaiah, Gideon, and a host of other biblical characters are remembered more for the powerful impact of their service to God than for the powerful fuss they put up before making "yes" their final answer. And with many of them, "final" was a relative term. Reluctance often returned, sometimes with a vengeance. Well into his career, Jeremiah was ready to call it quits as a prophet but for a certain fire in his bones that would not allow him to be silent. Jonah sulked and simmered as much *after* doing God's bidding as he did before first capitulating to the call following that infamous swallow test. As the flagship apostle, Peter signed on, then off, then on, then off, then on. We call him the Rock, by which we surely mean one of those novelty stones such as the one my sister once gave me that has the word "NO" etched into one side and "YES" into the other.

E. Stanley Jones wrote that "a person is not strong who does not bear within themselves antitheses strongly marked." He must have understood that only when we are fully awake to the cost of being a disciple can we again and again surrender faithfully and forcefully to that discipleship. *Although I could do otherwise, I will follow.* If the hatched pattern posed by the overlaying of our "no" with our "yes" takes the form of a cross, so be it. It was to be so for Jesus. During his ministry, he told a story about a son who said no to his father regarding work responsibilities, then changed his mind, at which point reluctance turned to virtue. I wonder if Jesus recalled that particular story when, in the garden before his arrest, he revealed his own reluctance to do his Father's bidding, followed by his unfathomable surrender: "Abba, Father, for you all things are possible; remove this cup from me; yet, not what I want, but what you want" (Mark 14:36).

I remember vividly a powerful reluctance that on one hot August day held me riveted for the longest time to the edge of the 10-meter platform at the public swimming pool in Kerrville, Texas. I was a young teenager on vacation with my family, and the pool was the perfect playground for my siblings and me. That towering platform called our name, and we had not been at the pool long at all before my younger brother and I climbed its zigzag staircase, moved to the platform's edge, and . . . paused to consider what to do next. We spent a good deal of time in that *paused to consider* mode—a favorite pastime of those deciding for or against any given leap of faith. Every once in a while we would shuffle sideways and back just slightly to make room for another swimmer who had climbed to the platform with the intention of actually jumping from it. Included among them was our older brother, who had taken his first plunge with none of this same hesitation, and who by now had progressed to swan diving off the platform as if there were no tomorrow.

As for me, ambivalence held sway, two forces pulling at me—gravity, and some other, more nebulous force. Common sense?

Cowardice? The survival instinct? I only knew two things: I wanted to jump, and at the same time I didn't. My younger brother and I talked through all the possibilities of each of these wants as we stood there with our toes curled over the concrete edge. We had already negotiated, with little trouble, the 1-meter and 3-meter diving boards. If only there were a 5-meter platform to climb to next, then a six, and a seven. . . . The leap from three to ten seemed overlarge. What were those city planners thinking? I peered down into that shimmering blue water, searching for some sign; all I saw was the reflection of a yawning sky. My reluctance deepened.

If you're not sure you're prepared to give your life wholly over to God, then go ahead and protest. Such reluctance is a sure identifier of just the sort of person God is known to employ. In fact, your protest is a likely sign you are on a forward course to meeting God, even though you appear to be running away. Chances are you are merely sprinting in the opposite direction down the aisle of a train you've already boarded for home. By even your best athletic efforts, you may make it all the way to the caboose and change by a few seconds your arrival into the station; given the exertion required by your efforts, you may also want to change your shirt once you get there.

Likewise, if you have shared your personal faith with a person searching for God and met with thoughtful resistance, consider that resistance both a compliment and a complement to the faith you represent. To take time to decide for discipleship is to take seriously the legitimacy of its demands as well as its rewards, something that can only be done by drawing nearer and nearer to it. As we have seen, some of God's most faithful servants have carried a dimension of reluctance to the threshold of decision—and even beyond.

"Make me a captive, Lord, and then I shall be free. Force me to render up my sword, and I shall conqueror be." The time-kept paradox that George Matheson captured and released so beautifully in meter and rhyme is that freedom and obedience are not two separate choices after all but two sides of the coin of the realm we know as life with God. With surrender to the call of God upon our lives comes true freedom, and not otherwise.

If the lifeguard on duty took amusement from the predicament of these two teenage boys camped out on the high plains of the 10-meter platform, after a while he also took pity. Up the stairs he climbed, then crossed over to where we stood at the platform's edge, introducing himself as John. Lifeguards, I always assumed, are trained to get you *out* of the water when you are in trouble, not the opposite. Nevertheless, John talked to us the way I am told those who are so gifted whisper a saddle onto a skittish horse. He told us what was true, that to jump was certainly scary, but that he would be at the pool's edge in case we needed him; and he told us what was probably not altogether true, that it was only water and what could water do but give way to us when we landed in it. God was with us, he added, and we need not be afraid. I didn't thank John at the time for giving the situation a spiritual dimension. Nobody enjoys being reminded that their fear of leaping is inversely related to their trust in God.

John had helped us establish the boundaries of our reluctance. He was only doing what advocates do, summoning us toward the very leap of faith we had been summoning toward ourselves. Every one of us wants somehow to prove or disprove the claim of Matheson's lines of verse—that to give ourselves wholly to God is to be free, to lay down the sword of our resistance, to conquer. Whether we will always admit it, we live for opportunities to do so. Jones's antitheses had been strongly marked in my brother and me, and we were the stronger for it.

No sooner had John resumed his place on the lifeguard stand than my brother slid his toe a little further off the edge of the platform than he had before. I did the same. His foot followed suit, and the next instant he was stepping onto an imaginary stair just beyond the platform, and I after him, matching his newfound sense of daring with my own.

As I broke the water's surface and rocketed downward into the silence of its depths, I was grinning ear to ear. The water that enveloped me so fully and completely felt utterly refreshing, even life-giving. Captive now to this immense body of blue, I was finally free of my fear of it. I felt I had been born again, born from above, as it were. Ten meters up, to be precise.

No sooner had my brother and I each surfaced than we were out of the pool and climbing those 10-meter platform steps again, dripping wet and laughing all the way to the top. We spent what was left of that August afternoon jumping, climbing, and jumping again. When no becomes yes, however long it takes, however many times the smooth stone must be turned back over again from one side to the other, then whatever the obstacles, the resistance, the original fear, the continuing reluctance, a floodgate is opened, and there is no preventing the rush of water from spreading as wide as it will over the waiting terrain as it claims then quenches every last thirst in its path.

part three

Whispering in the world

I disappear from the world as an object of
interest in order that I may be everywhere
in hiddenness and compassion.

Thomas Merton

The experience of prayer and the habits of the heart—what we might define as two aspects of the interior life—have been our subject up to now as we have put our ear to the Bible's pages and listened for the whisper of what is true. We have discovered that this interior life, while deeply personal, is never entirely private; that just as a whisper makes us think of two, so does God. For even in the realm of personal encounter with God we are inevitably brought around to the myriad and many-splendored ways we grow to relate to God within the fullness of human and creation community. Once we make that discovery, and the heart has made a place both for the God who loves the world and the world so loved, turning outward in love begins. We meet again on other terms the world that once we held at bay. When a child in the swimming pool dives to retrieve a coin that has been tossed to the bottom for his amusement, he lingers only briefly in that enchanted underwater realm before returning, coin in hand, to the loud and noisy surface—and not only for oxygen's sake.

The third dimension of the life of faith is our returning to the surface, beholding a second time the world we were born to love in all its pain and promise, noisiness and need, having been newly gifted with eyes to see it both deeply wounded and seeded in hope. As we do so, Jesus of Nazareth will lead us. For Jesus' life was the faithful rendering of unconditioned love—prayer flowing into pilgrimage, compassion into courage, a merciful heart into healing hands. In him we cannot know the dancer from the dance, so seamless in his life is the union of self-understanding and self-giving. His ministry is redemptive both through the grace of his life, death, and resurrection, and in the example of love he lived out for us to follow. It is his example that I hope will guide these next pages, and in a similar way, guide the ways we learn to live beyond them; that is to say, learn to lead and serve at a whisper in the world.

Chapter 11

The sincerity of the Messiah

He will not . . . cry aloud,
nor will anyone hear his voice in the streets.
Matthew 12:19

As a teenager I was drawn to singer Glen Campbell's rendition of "I Knew Jesus before He Was a Superstar." The reason the song spoke to me at that particular time in my life was partly because it contained chords I knew how to play on my guitar. But it also spoke to me because of its implication that, whatever had happened previously in the long, pending history of Christianity, Jesus had just now finally come into his own. He had reached the big time, earned the praise of the popular crowd, and most impressive of all, gained the admiration of big-name performing artists like Glen Campbell. Jesus had become a superstar.

Upon reflection, I have to admit that my enthusiasm may have been slightly overreaching. Jesus was not then nor is he yet the superstar of universal adulation and appeal the song implies. The fact is that every time he gets some momentum going in that direction—a nice rock opera in his honor, a "Jesus movement" following, a famous athlete or movie star going public with their faith—something happens, and the momentum slowly peters out. In my opinion, there is at least one simple reason: Jesus possesses a certain characteristic inhospitable to sustained stardom: *sincerity.*

The word "sincere" means genuine, absent any pretense, and free of deceit; it derives from the same word as "heart." To be sincere is, to borrow a phrase from the Beatitudes, to be pure in heart. Even so, sincerity is a virtue sometimes no more appreciated in its observance than in its breach. To be labeled sincere is often a patronizing gesture, as in "The poor thing—he means well. He is so sincere." For playmakers and power-mongers sincerity is the kiss of death. If you are wanting to expand your territory, move on an opportunity to gain a foothold for advancement, bend the rules just a little to con-venience or benefit yourself, engage in humor at another's expense, or simply cut loose and have a little fun on a Friday night, the last thing you need in your talent pool is sincerity.

Jesus, it turns out, is hopelessly sincere. He attends sabbath services religiously—and yet not to build a strong base of polit-ical support but simply because it is his custom (Luke 4:16). He tells the truth wherever he goes, even when it is not the least bit advantageous to do so. He resists every effort to draw a crowd around him to admire his wonders, as though compas-sion itself were reason enough to heal the sick, feed the hungry, or exorcise a demon. He speaks openly of his reliance on God, calling him his heavenly Father, and even "Daddy." Once, when he learns of a close friend's death, he cries—in public. He memorizes his Bible, spends time with children, and makes a habit of marveling at nature.

At a culminating moment in his ministry, Jesus removes whatever bloom may have been left on the rose of political opportunity by engaging in the combined equivalent of chang-ing a diaper, carrying out the trash, and unstopping a clogged drain. He is having supper with his disciples when he excuses himself, takes off his outer robe, wraps a towel around his waist, and begins to wash their feet. Imagine it—these men have been walking dusty roads in sandals (we hope) for who knows how long. And now Jesus is taking on the job of acknowledging their every step as he washes the dust and dirt from those twenty-four filthy, calloused feet. I think it goes without saying that the towel's best days are behind it.

What we discover is that Jesus is not doing this curious thing for dramatic effect but *sincerely*. This is a promotional opportunity like no other, but he cannot see it that way. "Wash all of me!" Peter intones, perhaps thinking to play up the sensational possibilities of the moment—at least for himself. "Why would I wash all of you?" Jesus answers, as if to say, "This is not about drama—it's about love. Now stop carrying on and let me wash your feet."

In a world in which the language and philosophy of marketing for consumption have deeply influenced the ways we speak and think about not only our own lives but also our communities of faith, Jesus raises a different sort of banner, one that looks for all the world like a wet and grimy towel. Sincerity of the sort Jesus demonstrates throughout his ministry draws upon a core identity to evaluate every presenting opportunity, rather than setting aside his identity for the appeal of that opportunity. Since Jesus' core identity is to love, he does not promote in order to gain; he serves in order to give.

The Jesus of the Gospels is not particularly methodical in subverting efforts to mold him for promotional purposes. He simply is who he is, neither sufficiently syrupy for the sweet nor sinewy for the stern, neither conservative enough for reactionary thinkers nor iconoclastic enough for radical thinkers. In the Bible that presents him to us, he is neither a bleeding heart nor a proponent of tough love. He's all for new wine, but protective of old wineskins. He both challenges political authority and supports it. He claims that his mission is to the house of Israel, but routinely widens his reach beyond that circle of kin.

He is respectful toward customs and rules, but breaks them as he deems appropriate. All this he does not in tactical, premeditated, or calculating ways but—here's that word again—sincerely, simply fulfilling his core identity and call from his heavenly Father.

The problem with being sincere is not only that living by principle is inherently difficult but also that you tend to disappoint a lot of people in the process. In this regard, Jesus *doesn't* disappoint. His family, his disciples, the Pharisees, the Sadducees, the scribes, the crowds, the Roman authorities—all find Jesus, at one time or another, a vexing figure. As we know, he eventually becomes too vexing to tolerate. Let's be honest: the sincere are difficult to trust. They are bound to say or do that which popular opinion would agree is the wrong thing at the wrong time simply because they believe it to be the right thing at the right time. Any parent can recall scenarios when their child was too far out of arm's reach to silence when they suddenly began to speak truthfully in a public setting about an embarrassing family situation or habit. Children soon enough acquire the talent of skirting a subject or bending the truth, having come to learn that honesty can be inconvenient, awkward, or even hurtful. Sincerity, as we have said, can be problematic in a world tooled for subliminal communication and contrived perceptions.

If, on the other hand, your child is facing surgery, your car has broken down by the road at night, or you are kneeling at the altar rail in an empty sanctuary on a weekday afternoon because you can no longer bear the weight of your guilt standing up, sincerity is no longer naive or well-meaning; it is all that matters. You want genuine assistance, and you want it mercifully given. As you look into the eyes of that surgeon, that passerby, that pastor who quietly walks into the sanctuary and kneels beside you, you couldn't care less whether they'd be a fun partner on a Friday night, but you very much need for them to be sincere.

The church has tried studying with those schooled in the science and art of packaging products for promotion and persuasion. We find appealing the idea that we can borrow from experts in that field to do a more effective job of selling ourselves. Our reasoning is that if these methods work for car batteries, why not for the church? What we have learned in the process of forming such alliances is that on a good day we are rather awkward in attempting to "get ourselves out there" with such promotional tools. Our "product" is as resistant to such efforts as the person of Jesus himself. And whenever we have grown less awkward and more nimble with these tools, the product we are so successfully promoting begins to be increasingly less recognizable as church. How plausible is a community of footwashers that attempts to bathe tired feet and sound brass trumpets at one and the same time? If we are advised to heal the sick and feed the hungry on stage so as to appeal by our compassion to the outside world, how will we adjust for the fact that compassion tends to eschew bright lights? What keeps us, finally, from starting to understand ourselves less and less theologically and more and more strategically, metamorphosing from church to product, successful perhaps, and well rated, but a consumable good rather than a community of faith? Jesus' words about gaining the world and losing our soul, while normally applied to the individual, may be a word to the church as well.

Our biggest concern, however, has yet to be mentioned. It is a concern for the heart of the one seeking God. At a moment of dread, tenderness, or wonder, when a person suddenly cares not a whit about sophistication or polish but needs desperately to look into a collective pair of eyes and find sincerity, what will they find when they look into ours? When we share our faith with a friend, neighbor, coworker, or stranger; when our congregations open their doors in hospitality and welcome, is it for the sake of the other that we take from the treasury the gift of good news, or for our own? A fine line exists between invitation, the very heart of the gospel, and self-promotion. As I understand these two, the first has the good of the other at heart, and reaches out for the sake of love; the second has our own benefit in mind, and the goal of self-preservation or self-enhancement. It is the whisper of invitation, not the shout of self-promotion, that the promotion-weary world waits so desperately to hear. Which will we offer? How can we seek to be more genuinely invitational and less self-promoting in who we are and how we share the faith? When we are willing even to ask these questions honestly of ourselves and one another, then we have already demonstrated something of the sincerity of Jesus.

In one of the many intriguing scenarios in the Gospels, Matthew tells us that Jesus is wishing to avoid notice from the Pharisees because of their plans to destroy him (see Matthew 12:14-15). He has healed the sick in a certain region, then immediately warns the people not to reveal him publicly. Matthew then quotes a phrase from Isaiah regarding the "Suffering Servant," a figure who will not "cry aloud, / nor will anyone hear his voice in the streets. / He will not break a bruised reed / or quench a smoldering wick / until he brings justice to victory. / And in his name the Gentiles will hope" (12:19-20). Matthew is clearly explaining Jesus' desire to avoid detection from his enemies. But he is also suggesting that by Jesus' hushing admonition to the crowds he is fulfilling the prophesy of Isaiah that the Suffering Servant, often considered to be the anticipated Messiah, will be both soft-spoken and forceful, both gentle in the minutest detail and global in his reach. He will work under the radar rather than on a stage, and his principal means of winning justice will be tenderness and mercy rather than power and prestige.

The longing earth waits for such a strong and gentle presence. Having seen such gentle strength once in the person of

Jesus, the world hopes to see more, this time in the lives and life together of those who go by his name. Among the ways the followers of Jesus collectively practice faith is this way: whispering to the world the love of God that has first been whispered to us. If Isaiah had it right, if Jesus had it right, it is just such a whisper that will both right the toppled flower and redeem the world.

Chapter 12

Two hands

But this one thing I do . . .
Philippians 3:13

The Gospels present us with a portrait of a Messiah who does not speak from the top down but whose compassion moves instead from the ground up. He understands his ministry not in terms of "empiring" but emptying, identifying himself principally as "one who serves" (Luke 22:27). In him the glory of God finds its expression in the lowest places, demonstrated most vividly in washing the disciples' feet. He subsequently summons us to live as he has lived, to serve as he has served. "So if I, your Lord and Teacher, have washed your feet, you also ought to wash one another's feet" (John 13:14).

I have participated many times over the years in the ritual act of footwashing, as the congregations I served gathered on Holy Thursday around a basin of water with a towel to serve one another and be served. The pairings have been, year after year, unspeakably tender—an elderly man bending to wash the feet of a child, a rambunctious little boy growing miraculously subdued as he washes his mother's feet with surprising tenderness, a businesswoman rolling up the stained trousers of a boarding house resident before lifting his feet into the basin of warm water. On Holy Thursday some years ago two congregations—one Hispanic, the other primarily Anglo—met together to share the ritual. As feet were washed that night, an entire history of complicated relationships across two cultures was salved and simplified by the mere gesture of feet held in hand, washed, and dried, followed by the *abrazo*, a holy embrace.

Washing feet calls for several things. An eye for clean is helpful, along with a stiff upper lip; love, of course, of the durable sort; water, a basin, and a towel; and most important, two hands. In all my years of participating in footwashing, I have yet to see a person with two hands not use both for the washing of feet.

I learned the importance of using two hands for a caring task not on a Holy Thursday evening in the sanctuary but on a spring day in the backyard of the church parsonage. Our daughter, Anna, three years old at the time, was my playmate for the afternoon while the older two children were off on an errand with their mother. I had brought the cordless telephone into the yard, setting it on a small table next to where I stood pushing Anna in her favorite swing. Pastors learn early on the importance of efficiency. Should the phone ring, I could answer it while still attending to Anna.

It rang. To this day I cannot remember who called. What I do remember is that as I reached for that phone, so cleverly placed within arm's length of the swing set, I continued to push Anna with one hand as I answered the call with the other. No sooner had I said "Hello" than Anna called from her swing, "Two hands, Daddy!"

Anna's words have accompanied me through all the years that have followed. They have affected the way I pastor, preach, and preside at font and table, and the way I teach others to do so. They have influenced my efforts to negotiate a balance between church and home, work and rest, prayer and activity, time in the parish and time spent working at my desk or in the study. Those words have deepened my prior understanding of Jean-Pierre De Caussade's notion of "the sacrament of the present moment." The subject of an entire book by this eighteenth-century French Jesuit priest was explained to me in three words by a toddler in a swing: two hands, Daddy!

Multitasking has been welcomed into our postmodern lifestyles with all the hospitality reserved for our most trusted friends. Gadgets and devices, in combination with a heightened sense of immediacy with regard to our personal and professional responsibilities, leave us attempting, more and more of the time, to function and relate at multiple levels at once. It is as though once our trusted friends have arrived, we attempt to attend to each one individually while at the same time going about our usual routines, diminishing every relationship in the process. The sense of self-importance reinforced by such behavior is plain, if largely unacknowledged. But even less frequently do we recognize another subtle motive for gathering multiple tasks and conversations around us like a nervous hyena gather her litter: the adrenaline effect derived from the intensity of such ramped-up, doubled-up activity. In essence, we are using one another to rev ourselves out of community.

Seldom do we stop to wonder if dividing our attention so extensively is a faithful way to live. Of course we can talk on the phone and push a child in the swing at the same time, but *should* we? Nor do we generally ask whether some things are worth waiting for even if they can be obtained immediately. Of course we and others are available, accessible, and able to respond, if not immediately, then within minutes of a call, text message, or e-mail, but *should* we be? *Must* we be? Finally, we seem largely content with having our thoughts and activities constantly derailed by interruptions. Even though we are physically capable of jumping the tracks at a moment's notice, are such continual interruptions (the word means to rupture or break, as in "break my concentration") really good for our souls, our relationships, or the larger work and quality of life of the community? When Nietzsche observed in the nineteenth century that what was needed in heaven and on earth was "long obedience in the same direction," could he have possibly imagined the twenty-first-century application of his observation on a scale of seconds and minutes rather than years and lifetimes?

Age quod agis. "Do what you are doing." It is a maxim among the Jesuits, the same order to which De Caussade belonged. If we consider the nature and scope of Jesus' ministry, we see him proving time and time again the worth and wisdom of this saying. "With two hands," whether understood figuratively or literally, describes the whole of his work—as well as the work to which he has called those who follow him. Jesus was certainly busy, and interrupted, as are we—those are characteristics of living with a sense of social responsibility. Yet, in the midst of those realities, what would it mean for us to practice greater deliberateness in our lives so as to allow us, to the best of our ability, to "do what we are doing"? Perhaps a greater wakefulness and "waitfulness" throughout the day to listen with the heart for the still, small voice; encountering others in what Martin Buber once called "I-Thou" rather than "I-It" ways, that is, with genuine attentiveness and regard; embarking on the patient work of shared discernment in complex or ambiguous decision-making, both at home and in congregational and community life; and openness in general to those small epiphanies that appear like lightning bugs along our dusky paths. Included in this latter awareness would be noticing the lightning bugs themselves, and all of nature with them, with both heart and mind open to enchantment by nature's wonders, acceptance of its ordinariness, and respect for its fragility. These are the everyday callings inviting us to present ourselves with both hands to that which is before us, that is, to do what we are doing. Last but foremost, Scripture waits for its depths to be plumbed, its riches mined, its wisdom revealed by those who will hold that sacred text in both hands, sitting alone and together before a single verse, a single story, a single book long enough for earthquake, fire, and wind to pass, and a fresh whisper to be heard through those ancient words.

"This one thing I do . . ." Paul wrote to the church at Philippi. Before we ever follow the sentence forward from there, in this one phrase we have already had presented to us, with two hands, the wisdom of the ages: that life at its best is to do one thing, the best thing for the time being, and to bring to that moment's work the presence and attentiveness of an apostle—that is, one who has been *sent* for precisely this purpose. The world is replete with appeals, invitations, seductions, ambitions, and promises. To welcome these interruptions is to change the tally in Paul's phrase from "this *one* thing" to "these *few* things," then "many," then "myriad," until finally we arrive at "legion," a word recalling a certain tortured figure Jesus once encountered who was racked with too many demons to number, all tugging on him at once (see Mark 5:1ff). E-mails, phone calls, text messages, billboards, weather alerts, commercial fragments, and news flashes run amok.

The church has an antidote for overtasking, a mostly overlooked treasure hidden in plain view within its yearly calendar. We call it "Ordinary Time." On the calendar, Ordinary Time occurs in two places; it comes in one long stretch between Pentecost in the Northern Hemisphere's spring and Reign of Christ Sunday in the fall, just prior to Advent; and in one short stretch between Epiphany (January 6) and the beginning of Lent. Ordinary Time means just what it says—that the time is ordinary, routine, characterized by the absence of high feasts and dramatic cycles such as Christmas and Easter. If the Christian year has a voice, then Ordinary Time is its whisper.

For being so unscintillating a concept, Ordinary Time has much to commend it—especially in a noisy world. It speaks, quietly, of the legitimacy of the plain, the value of the regular, the importance of the familiar. It is time's understated invitation to practice that "long obedience in the same direction" Nietzsche believed was so needed. These are among the lessons to be learned from those two curious stretches of weeks on the Christian calendar that are no specific time, and no day in particular.

Further, being an unscintillating concept is precisely what makes Ordinary Time so instructive. The season resists hype and persuasion like the ocean doldrums resist a sail. There is nothing about it to pitch or promote, nothing to harness or bottle or package and carry to market. Just plain old, garden-variety ordinary time. The fact that the season is the longest on the calendar, encompassing more than half the year, speaks to the fact that life's long stretches of level ground are to be embraced as fully as its mountaintops, and walked as attentively as its valleys. Wide open spaces on the sacred calendar serve to remind us that there are also, if we allow it to be so, wide open spaces in the mind and heart.

The appeal of God to be in relationship with us waits to be heard and apprehended in all its understated breadth and scope. With two unfettered hands literally left to their own devices, we possess the freedom to relate to God and others incidentally, offhandedly, in a string of "I-It" relationships; or deliberately, carefully, earnestly, in "I-Thou" relationship. For the latter purpose, both hands are called for.

So reach for your bookmark, and put this book aside. Then open your hands. Turn them in the direction of whatever ordinary thing is before you. Hold a too-familiar face in those two hands and call it dear. Fold those hands together and call it prayer. Do as Jesus did and enfold the children within your reach, one at a time, blessing each in turn. Do the dishes, or

drive to work; call a friend, or write a letter; ride a bike, or prepare a lesson; turn a somersault, or just breathe as you watch
the unveiling of the night sky. Wash the feet of those who have
walked a long, dusty way to encounter such a witness, such a
way of life, such a love as has learned how with two hands to do
just one thing.

Chapter 13

A cantilevered life

*How beautiful are the feet of those
who bring good news . . .*
Romans 10:15b

In 1936 the Kaufmann family of Pittsburgh decided they were
ready to develop land they owned east of the city in that
beautiful area of western Pennsylvania known for its rolling
hills and lush forests. The family had a basic idea of the spot
where they wanted to build what would be their summer home
and weekend getaway. A respectable stream known as Bear
Run, complete with a cascading thirty-foot waterfall, mean-
dered through the property. Just downstream from that waterfall was a generous plot of level ground with a marvelous view
of the falls. Imagine it as the Kaufmanns surely did: a bay window right there in the living room so that morning and evening
they could witness that majestic scene of water vaulting over
the rock ledge before plunging into the pool below. Friends
invited from the city for the evening or the weekend would be
utterly transfixed as they stood in the living room and took in
that marvelous view. The guest book would read like a prayer
book.

I stood on that very site some years ago, taking in the view of that upstream waterfall as though a guest in the Kauffmanns' home. The Kaufmanns were right—it was the perfect place for their summer home to be built. I looked around for the guest book to register my own prayer of awe and thanks, but there was no prayer book. In fact, there was no living room. The place where I stood was, well, a vacant lot.

The architect the Kaufmanns asked to design their house was Frank Lloyd Wright, already very well regarded at the time, and also known for his tendency toward the capricious. Wright took the commission, and while the Kaufmann family was going about their business in Pittsburgh, he was drawing up the plans for their retreat home. In doing so, his sense of architectural license got the better of him. He decided the location the Kaufmanns had chosen for the house—the one with the spectacular view of the falls—was less than ideal.

He proceeded to design a house that would be situated upstream and on its opposite bank, extending above the very waterfall the owners had in mind to admire from that beautiful setting downstream. The house Wright designed was to be anchored into the solid rock beside the stream and suspended in midair as it projected out over the water.

The resulting structure was given the name "Fallingwater." To tour that home today is to walk into a house whose floor is situated virtually *on top of* the running stream. Step outside the living room and onto the patio, lean over the rail, and right below you, in lieu of a well-tended flower bed, is a rushing mass of water hurling itself over the ledge of a thirty-foot cliff. One sure way to lower your landscaping bill.

Wright was able to pull off what he did because of his expansive ego, but also because of a physics principle known as the cantilever. A cantilever is achieved when something is anchored *here* and reaches over *there*. It is a very simple concept, and we employ it constantly. Whenever we stretch out an arm, it is supported not by the air beneath it, but by the frame of the body from which it extends. When we bring our leg forward in order to take a step, we can do so only because the center of gravity is back with the rest of us—in our body's core. Without the cantilever principle, we would tumble to the floor every time we glanced at our watch or leaned in to hear a whisper.

The word *cantilever* literally means "lifting the edge," and that is surely what Frank Lloyd Wright did to the Kaufmanns when he presented them with plans to build their dream home over a waterfall! He lifted the edge of their lives, ruffled their sense of security, and subverted their assumptions, pouring cold water over any idea of admiring the waterfall from a safe distance. It is as though he said, "I want you to experience the swirling, churning, sweeping current of water not right before your eyes but right beneath your feet. You wanted to admire the water; I want you to make it your pillow."

I have this hunch that the Holy Spirit was trained in the same school of architecture as Frank Lloyd Wright. We or someone on our behalf says, "Yes, I will be a Christian." We draw near the font of baptism and by the cantilever principle are suspended over the water to receive that gift as a sign of God's grace in our lives; what we know less well is that the act is also a sign of things to come. We say, "That was great! Now that I am in the fold, over here is where I would like my house to be built. I want to be in on the things of God in a big way, as in a big picture window looking out over the new creation work. From here I will have a perfect vantage point for seeing all the good things God is doing in the world. What's more, I can stick my toe in the water whenever it suits me." The Holy Spirit nods; then, while we are going about our business, proceeds to build our house. When it is completed, it is bold and beautiful, sturdy and strong, but it is not on terra firma as we had planned it—it is over thin air. We put our foot down: "That is not what I had in mind!" The Holy Spirit responds, "The cantilevered moment of your baptism was not only a symbol—it was your new life in miniature."

Have you ever wondered why Paul, when he is writing about preaching in his letter to the Roman church, raises the subject of feet? "How are they to hear without someone to proclaim ..." he writes. Then "As it is written, 'How beautiful are the feet of those who bring good news!'" (Romans 10:14ff) Why feet? Why not, How beautiful are the *lips* ... How beautiful are the *voices* ... How beautiful are the *words* ...? There many things I strive to make beautiful as a preacher, a teacher, a writer, but I must say that feet have never been high on the list. Why feet?

Is it that feet are such draft horses in the day-in, day-out work of living the gospel? Whether we preach, pray, sing, dance, march for justice, cook for the hungry, teach, heal, raise children, or wash feet, feet are involved in the effort, and seldom noticed. Is this a moment for honorable mention of an unheralded part of the workforce?

Does Paul mention feet because preaching has as much to do with the preacher's entire lifestyle as with fifteen minutes of words and gestures? I have often asked my preaching students when the sermon begins. "At the first word," one will say. "When you get up from your seat," another offers. Pregnant pause. "When the service begins," a student suggests, breaking the silence. They are all correct, of course, but I don't comment just yet. "That morning, when you first enter the building and begin greeting people," someone surmises. Soon we realize that feet are directly related to proclaiming the good news. Where I go, what I do, how I think and speak and behave *between* sermons all becomes *part* of the sermon in ways that may be invisible to me, but certainly not to others. If we were to continue our little game, the answers would back up from Sunday morning all the way to baptism, the moment at which we or someone we know presented us to God for keeps. Still dripping with water, we became and will never cease to be a beacon to the redeeming power of grace in the lives of those whose lives belong to God.

Paul may have in mind the original context for the reference—Isaiah's poetic declaration to the exiles in Assyria of their imminent release: How beautiful are the feet that carry to your door the good news of your liberation and return to Zion, your once and future home. When someone brings good news at a moment we most desperately need it, everything about them—feet, nose, pointy ears—becomes instantly and for all time beautiful.

Paul's words could mean any of these things, and possibly one thing besides: That to put one foot in front of the other for the gospel cause is to live a cantilevered life, every step its own mini-leap of faith. To go into the world—or even the family room, for that matter—guided by the love of Christ is to step out in faith, trusting unseen realities "to keep you from falling," as the letter of Jude puts it. How beautiful are the feet, the hands, the thoughts, the dreams, the deeds of the one who dares to venture from the safety and security of home base and cantilever into the great unknown regions that lie beyond the usual borders of their gravity-bound self.

The Holy Spirit assures us that any time we are willing to step into that house, that life, that calling we are given at our baptism, and then do so again, and again, we will be grounded, as Archbishop Fulton Sheen once put it, by "invisible means of support," means beyond what we can possibly imagine. God will never fail to secure that foundation, even as we step out in new ways to live boldly and beautifully in Christ.

The waters are stirring today, as they do every day and even in the night, as though on a mission, a swiftly moving current set on sweeping you off your feet and into life. Draw near, or keep your distance—the call of God would be the dictate of God if it ever ceased to present us with both choices. Hire a more compliant architect and build your house downstream. Begin even now to imagine the arrangement of your living room furniture for the best view, the friends you will have over, the guest book you will encourage them to sign as they leave so you can later enjoy their written expressions of admiration and awe.

Or . . . step into the house someone we know and love was daring enough to build right over the rushing stream as an emblem of your baptism. Make the bedrock your rock bed, the water your pillow. And on each new morning as you swing your feet over the bedside in your first cantilevered act of the day, let this be your prayer: May every step I take today, including this very prayer, be its own small leap of faith. Let me be so grounded in the awareness of your love and provision that my heart and hands reach toward every needed place, and upward in praise and thanksgiving, not hindered by fear of falling, but freely and with joy. If in this trust walk I cannot always be certain of my way, then let me be assured of your presence. May I see in every surrendering step your gift to me, and mine to you, of this cantilevered life.

Chapter 14

The whisper
beneath the shout

Bear fruits worthy of repentance.
Luke 3:8a

The story of John the Baptist is usually read in congregational worship in December, during the season of Advent as we draw near Christmas. John, as you recall, is in the wilderness when the word of God comes to him. Matthew and Mark tell us he is clothed with camel's hair and eats locusts and wild honey. He begins to preach, and crowds begin to form. "Repent!" is the message most closely associated with this desert prophet, a word that means to change directions or turn around. Forgiveness also finds its way into his sermons, as does the nearness of God's kingdom. Not a bad set of themes for a preacher with somewhat limited access to illustrations.

The Gospel of Luke contributes significantly to what we know about the content of John's prophetic message. "Bear fruits worthy of repentance," John tells the people (Luke 3:8a). In other words, if you leave this desert claiming to have "turned around," then concrete changes should be evident in your lives. Remarkably, the crowds are not scared away by this elaboration of the message but seem instead to draw even nearer to this strange prophet. In response to his challenge, they ask what we might consider a universal moral and spiritual question: "What then should we do?"

This is where the stories of John in Luke's Gospel fit in so nicely with our idea of Christmas charity, at least ostensibly so. John's answer to the "what should we do" question is to lend a hand to help the poor: "Whoever has two coats must share with anyone who has none; and whoever has food must do likewise" (Luke 3:11ff). As if taking our cue from John, December moves us into overdrive with efforts to provide the less fortunate with gift baskets, turkey dinners, school supplies, blankets, coats, toys, visits from Santa, and on and on.

I have participated in and even presided over many of these Advent and Christmas projects during my years as a pastor. You and I could trade stories of poignant moments resulting from bringing Christmas to an underprivileged family. These projects are often beautiful expressions of love and care. But I do not believe they are precisely what John is talking about.

John is firmly rooted in what we call the prophetic tradition of ancient Israel. That tradition represents a long history of divine messengers disturbing the comfortable and comforting the disturbed, raising either a cry of "Woe to you . . ." or a call of "Comfort, comfort . . ." depending on the circumstance. The message of these prophets is so basic it could almost be a kindergarten lesson. The list of things that really matter to them numbers two: devotion to God and a just society. One prophet may emphasize the first, another, the second, but both themes are found in virtually every message. In fact, what we discover is that the two are so intertwined as to be inseparable. To love God is to be led to doing and describing justice, just as to treat the neighbor and stranger fairly is to honor God.

As with the prophets who went before him, John doesn't deal with this vision cosmetically. As one who speaks for God, he is after more than charity; he wants justice too. In other words, a turkey dinner and a toy drive will not suffice. Root causes of poverty and marginalization must be identified and addressed. Let's look more closely at the direction he gives those who ask what they should do to get beyond turkeys and toys.

Whoever has two coats must share with anyone who has none, and whoever has food must do likewise. I will volunteer in an instant to buy *another* coat or *another* can of sweet corn for someone who has none, but when you start reaching into *my* closet or cupboard to give away some of what is already mine, sorry, John—now you've quit preaching and gone to meddling.

Meddling is precisely what John wants to be doing. He is reminding the crowds, and any of us who happen to overhear, that justice is not about seeing that those who live at the margins of society have a happy holiday by spilling into their apartments bearing gifts from the discount store. Justice is rearranging things so that those who have too many coats in their closet get delivered of that curse while those who have none receive the blessing of a survivable winter. That is the sort of fruit John wants to see borne by a community of faith that is equally distressed by both material excess and material deficiency.

Now that our feathers are ruffled, let's have a look at what John wants from the tax collector and the soldier: *Collect no more than the amount prescribed for you . . . Do not extort money from anyone by threats or false accusation . . .* What John is asking, essentially, is for these two groups to relinquish the special privileges to which their respective professions have entitled them. Both tax collectors and soldiers wield power over the common people—that's part of the attraction of jobs that otherwise entail plenty of hazards. If they refrain from exploiting that power, they earn a bureaucrat's humble wage, a soldier's meager pay—nothing to write home about. Both can get rich quick by choosing otherwise.

Furthermore, tax collectors and soldiers in a culture of corruption would be expected by their peers to abide by certain codes of extortionary conduct. The tax collector who decides to play fair has made a decision, by extension, *not* to play fair with his cohorts. They, in turn, are certain to be both peeved at and threatened by this renegade who thinks he's better than everybody else. Same with the soldier. With a little imagination, you may be able to identify a setting in your own life that fits this description. John is asking the nearly impossible: choose to have your wages decimated and your insider status jeopardized, all for the sake of some spiritual quest, all for the sake of God.

Let's be clear about the fact that justice is an extension of mercy, not its opposite. The prophets would encourage providing dinner for a struggling family. But they would go on to challenge us to ask what is behind the struggle, and to help resolve it, even if it leads to challenging an unfair system; *even* if it leads to acknowledging our own part in it. When it comes to the relationship of mercy, justice, and honoring God, the prophet Micah said it best: "And what does the Lord require? The Lord has shown you, O mortal, what is good: to do justly, love mercy, and walk modestly with your God" (Micah 6:8, translation mine). Justice, mercy, and a relationship with God are not three different paths by which to choose to live out our faith; they are different lanes on the very same road, the path leading toward God's new society.

John does not despise his listeners—he cares as much for them as for those desperate for a coat and a crust of bread. He simply understands that the prevailing culture will do virtually anything to overinflate our sense of our own worth by tying it to what we own and whom we order around. He also knows that to reject that insidious force is to be cut from puppeteer's strings. Establishing fairness finally means freedom for all involved. This is why, in summarizing John's seemingly severe wilderness tirade, Luke can use the words "exhortation" and "good news" in the same sentence: "So, with many other *exhortations*, [John] proclaimed the *good news* to the people" (Luke 3:18, emphasis mine).

This is also why, a sentence later, Herod throws John into prison. For to challenge the prevailing systems of affluence and influence, calling on one another to divest ourselves of some of our wealth and power for the sake of the poor, including our own poor souls, is to raise serious objections from those keenly vested in both wealth and power staying put. If charity is among the most roundly soothing concepts in the world, justice is its equal in creating unease. Dom Hélder Câmera, a Roman Catholic archbishop living in Brazil in the twentieth century, is famous for his observation that "when I give food to the poor, they call me a saint. When I ask why the poor have no food, they call me a Communist." Bestowing upon charity ministries the designation of first-order kingdom work can advance the fiction that our deeds of mercy are the ultimate goal of our discipleship. We then become inoculated from any concern for what should follow charity in the way of working with our poorer neighbors—and their working with us— toward lifestyles of modesty and adequacy for *both* of us. As long as I can afford to have two coats and buy a *third* for my neighbor, my own cooperation with society's code of consumerism is protected—even reinforced. I, the compassionate double-consumer, have had my cake and eaten it too. To say "Repent!" is to say, literally, "Enough!" a word guaranteed to create air turbulence at higher latitudes of acquisition and sway. John lost his life using such words as these; his cousin Jesus would eventually share the same fate.

The Reverend Marti Soper, a clergy friend, tells of a moment a few years ago when the congregation she serves gathered in a circle on Ash Wednesday to impose ashes on one another's foreheads. Marti initiated the imposition with the person beside her: "Repent, and believe the gospel," she said as she marked an ashen cross on their forehead. Around the room the ashes went, and with them those solemn words, "Repent, and believe the gospel," spoken in voices young and old, male and female, innocent and wise. Meanwhile, Andrew, who was ten years old, stood next to Pastor Marti patiently waiting his turn. "Pastor Marti, can I do you?" he whispered to her as the ashes were making their way around the circle. "Yes," she whispered back. Finally his turn came. Having been marked with the ashes, then handed the vessel, Andrew turned to Pastor Marti and made the sign of the cross on her forehead as he said, "Pastor Marti, *rebel* and believe the gospel."

Getting the words wrong in worship is not the worse thing in the world—especially if it means getting them right. As Andrew placed the sign of the cross on his pastor's forehead that night, he had spoken an ancient truth in a fresh way, for *rebel* is as close to repent as any word can be. To "turn around" or "change directions" is to question not only our own course but the very map society has given us to go by, as well as the grand machine that has designed that map, these latter two involving a different order of magnitude. This is what the Quaker tradition means by "speaking truth to power." The phrase should come with a caveat: no one who does so should expect a one-way conversation.

What we often miss in this desert drama is the desperation in the voices of John's listeners. No one forced these tax collectors, soldiers, and assorted others to traipse all the way into the wilderness in order to beg some catchpenny prophet with locust breath to make them truly alive. And yet they came. No one made them ask that universal moral and spiritual question, and yet they asked it: "What then should we do . . . ?" I can practically hear their desperation even as I voice those words myself. If you put those words on your own lips, I am quite certain you will hear it too.

John's shout in the wilderness is really a whisper in disguise, a compassionate plea for freedom offered to those as much in need of deliverance as repentance. For the fact is that most of us are caged by our lifestyles of consumption and preoccupation with possessing, and no less so for having the fancier cage, the costlier cage, the board-on-board fence cage, the all-leather interior cage, or the 14-carat cage. The desperation of the powerful is powerful indeed, the yearnings of the rich, rich with deep possibilities for knowing God and living near God through discovering an alternative way of being. All that is required for us to be powerfully, richly delivered into that divine relationship is a willingness to do just what Andrew did—the wrong thing that is really the right thing: repent, rebel, and live.

Chapter 15

Will work for food

*Do not work for the food that perishes, but for the food
that endures for eternal life.*
John 6:27a

Our generation of Americans is uniquely voracious. We consume more food than has any other civilization on the planet at any time in history. To give an idea of the scope of our appetites, here is what the average American eats over a lifetime: four tons of beef, four tons of potatoes, four tons of fresh vegetables, three-and-a-half tons of sugar, three tons of fresh fruit, two tons of chicken, a half ton of fish, a half ton of cheese, 2,000 gallons of milk, 2,000 gallons of soft drinks, 1,800 gallons of beer, 296 gallons of wine, 880 gallons of tea, 20,000 eggs, 108,000 slices of bread, and last but not least, 80,000 cups of coffee.

But we are equal opportunity consumers, not limiting ourselves to food. Michel Lotito was the kind of person who appeared in books that chronicle world records, but in other ways he was not so different from the rest of us. Over his lifetime, he ate lots of stuff besides food; to be specific, twelve bicycles, seven shopping carts, a metal coffin, a cash register, a washing machine, a television, and 660 feet of fine chain. His tastes grew more expensive over time. Giving new meaning to the phrase "fast food," he eventually ingested a four-seat air-craft, complete with its 2,500 pounds of aluminum, steel, vinyl, plastic, rubber, and various and sundry nuts and bolts.

The man who ate funeral coffins and airplanes was a curious sideshow, but he was, in another sense, a main-stage metaphor for our own society, with its unparalleled appetites for food, certainly, but also for things—things we may not eat, but nonetheless use up and throw away, or don't use up, then throw away: vehicles, appliances, houses, furniture, entertainment, packaging, rain forests, topsoil, and aquifers, to name a few. We have made the world our oyster, and as it slithers down our throat, we are already rooting in the mud for our next morsel.

In the last chapter we saw how, with his pointed challenge to the crowds who came out to see him, John the Baptist, to bor-row an image from the familiar world of processed food, opened a can of worms. And a can of worms is precisely what we feel we are holding after he is finished with us. The indul-gences and abuses of which he speaks seem foolish in his com-pany, childish, inordinately selfish. How did we who are standing here in this godforsaken desert seeking God grow to be so greedy, so inhumane, so empty of real purpose and mean-ing? The poor of our planet cry out for the simplest things—food and clean water. We do not hear their cries; our ears are busy identifying new consuming interests. We do not speak to their needs—our mouths are busy getting us to that life goal of four tons of beef. Those seeking to know the God of Christian faith turn to us for guidance, for a trustworthy witness to faith-ful life and devotion. Before we can utter a word in response, our lives and lifestyles speak on our behalf.

The crowds that are following Jesus through John's Gospel have just the day before been fed by his hand (John 6:1ff). It is such a phenomenal experience for them, they determine to take Jesus by force and make him king! Notice that it is not his teachings that inspire their response, or his healings, or his gestures of radical forgiveness. It is, plain and simple, his ad hoc cooking skills. Those must have been some pretty good barley loaves. He escapes from their ecstatic reveries, retreating first into the mountains, then across the lake. The following day, however, they succeed in tracking him down. He knows what's on their minds—they want to see the breakfast menu. "Do not work for the food that perishes," he tells them, "but for the food that endures for eternal life."

With the pairing of two sorts of "food" in the same sentence, Jesus provides us with a keen insight into human nature: there is a hunger in the heart that is so closely bound up, body and soul, with other hungers that we often confuse them. In other words, there's food, and then there's food. We feel an ache, and seek to satisfy it with a cheeseburger, a drink, an aspirin, an afternoon of shopping, or _____ [fill in the blank with your own remedy of choice]. The ache doesn't go away, but if we haven't addressed it, at least we have repressed it.

The ache, of course, is normally about something other than cheeseburgers. It has more to do with spiritual hungers that go unmet while we feed imaginary physical ones. Jesus' words to the crowds that came to him for breakfast are like a sword dividing fiction from truth: there's the food that perishes, and there's the food that endures. The former enjoys fairly well-established mechanisms for finding its way into your belly; the latter will require greater effort.

It is important to remember that Jesus honors the physical realm of life, heartily embracing the material world as the good and creative gift of God. But he does make obvious the fact that physical *indulgence* will tyrannize us to the point of destroying both our own lives and the lives of those for whom we are responsible. How shall we express compassion for the poor if we possess no sense of moderation or abstinence in our own lives? Further, how shall we invite others to "come and see" who Jesus is if our own appetites and lifestyles indicate that we have no need for him to be anything more than icing on the cake? Why would an inquirer into the faith be attracted to a figure of such modesty and simplicity if we who present him are not ourselves recognizable by those traits?

God is seeking a people who have had their fill of perishable living. Jesus is pursuing followers who demonstrate the tenacity to pursue him as these crowds did, but not because they are hungry for breakfast, instead because they hunger for the company of one so wise and good as he. The Holy Spirit yearns to breathe into us such a breath as will fill every hollow and hurting recess of our being, and so to make us whole in genuine rather than conjured ways, truly alive to the bountiful work and beautiful wonders for which God has created us.

This is the whisper that enters a world made loud with shouting of so many sorts, a whisper that yet hopes to be heard by each of us, and all of us together. These are the ways we learn to walk when we decide that God can be trusted to lead us to the water's edge, and even over. These are the disciplines we begin to practice when we awaken to the simple wonder and deep mystery of God's summoning call into relationship. Most of all, this is the way of life we grow to love when we discover that we are loved by God, and that we can believe this good news more than we believe our fear that it is not really so. Work for this food, Jesus says. And then, as if to contradict himself, he says, "I will give it to you" (John 6:27). I thought you said we had to work for it. "*This* is your work, the work of God within you: to believe in me" for all you need. It turns out that Jesus is the bread for which we truly hunger. To trust him to be so is the work we've been given; to trust him to be so is to be nourished for life.

The gift of God

If you knew the gift of God, and who it is that is saying to you, "Give me a drink," you would have asked him, and he would have given you living water.

John 4:10

Epilogue. Technically, it means the "after" word, the word *after* the last word—what is written once everything has been written. I find it very helpful for my own purposes. What the French call *l'esprit d'escalier*, staircase wit—deciding on the perfect words to say, but about three minutes too late; that is to say, while leaving by the staircase—has often been my inclination. Therefore, the opportunity for an epilogue is like a birthday in the middle of the year.

We know someone in the Bible for whom the opportunity for an epilogue is a birthday in the middle of her *life*. A Samaritan woman comes to draw water at a well where Jesus, bending at least one rule, and probably several, is loitering. He asks her for a drink of water. They talk briefly, and then he says to her, "If you knew . . . you would have asked . . . [I] would have given . . ." From these words we gather that an overture has been made, and missed. Whatever the offer was, it's too late now; the window of opportunity has closed; the last word has been written. If you knew . . . but no . . .

This has been a book of overtures. Scripture has presented itself to us in various ways, loitering at the water well, as it were, to ask of us a drink. Those Bible verses that began each chapter's conversations have provided the tiny sequence of epiphanies, blinking like lightning bugs to lure us out of our lawn chairs and into life. We have thought about prayer, considered the heart's habits, reflected on Jesus and the ways *we* may walk as he once did, learning to live lives of justice, mercy, and modesty. At each turning of a page of Scripture, we have been invited to take a cantilevered step right off the edge of that page and into the enveloping waters of new life.

We may have said "no" each time, or perhaps not even heard the whisper for all the clamor and commotion around us. We may find ourselves at the well with the Samaritan and Jesus feeling not so different than she—curious, intrigued, but at the moment looking up the wrong end of the miracle. If we knew the gift, we would have asked and been given; but no . . .

The good news is this: with God, there is always a word after the last word. In fact, it could be said that the church's principal responsibility to the world is to be the gospel's living epilogue. And for all the foibles and follies that mar the beauty and blessing of its call, it somehow manages to do so. Often, when the grace of God holds sway, the church speaks the truth in enough of a whisper to be heard beneath the din. In such moments, "If you knew the gift of God" is brought into the present tense, and becomes all epilogue: "You *can* know the gift of God. We can *together* know the gift of God."

What is this "gift of God" that we can know together? A set of rules? An updated laundry list of our shortcomings and areas needing improvement? Is the gift a set of instructions for how we must learn to pray, guide our hearts upward rather than downward, learn a way of whispering in the world? What is this gift that is said to be of God?

Our son, David, at five years of age, would occasionally accompany me to the nursing home to visit parishioners. The boy was all wonder at the wheelchairs, motorized beds, and extension grabbers that reached things one had not the where-withal to reach another way. He took on trade the rudimentary smells of aging humanity and the notable absence of anyone else remotely close to his age. As we walked the halls, every face that met his gaze lit up, charmed. David, it seemed to me, was his own best gift; I have no doubt the nursing home residents felt the same.

Miss Jesse Daniel was a favorite of his, and he of hers. On our visits to her room she would always have ready a small gift of some kind in case he happened to be along—a little wooden car, a piece of chocolate candy, a bookmark. One day we entered the room, and after hugging us both she gave him one of her little presents. Then, with the wink of her eye, she asked him, "What did you bring *me?*"

It is a fair question, and it is time we asked it of God. We have been giving what we can of attention, study, reflection, consid-eration. We have listened for the whisper beneath and beyond the pages of Scripture; the whisper in the church house, the whisper beneath the shout. Having come to the end of a book that has asked something of us at every turn, this turn should be ours. God, we have listened as carefully as we know how. We have brought you what we could; what did you bring *us?*

David didn't hesitate to answer Jesse's question. In the most straightforward way he simply said, "I brought you myself." She smiled broadly, and then they spent the next half hour or so laughing, telling stories, playing with extension grabbers, and eating chocolates before we left with a prayer and a prom-ise to return. David was true to his word—he had brought her himself. It is the gift we give before we learn to cultivate sub-stitutes, the gift best known to young children and God.

"If you knew the gift of God . . ." Jesus began. And she

hadn't. She had missed that final homebound train by seconds, let the crystal figurine slip through her fingers and fall to the floor, thought of the perfect words to say, but only on her way down the stairs and out the door. Only this saved her: that when it comes to love, God is all about the epilogue, meeting us at the bottom of the stairs, ready to listen as we say those perfect words.

After she has missed the moment, Jesus and the woman continue to talk, meandering toward another opportunity the way hikers move switchback up a mountain's face. Sometimes, when it is our second try, roundabout is the best way to arrive at God. And roundabout, she does. Then, laden with this palpable sense of good news regarding this mysterious figure who may just be the Messiah, she hurries back to the city to share her excitement. As she departs—and I find this the most poignant detail of the story—she leaves her water jar at the well. Is it in her haste that she has chosen not to bother with a vessel that would have been her lifeline? Is she so flustered by her encounter that she simply forgets it?

I like to believe she leaves her water jar behind because the gift that was almost missed has just now been offered again, and this time received, and who can think about water at a time like this? If you have known the experience of good news so gratifying, so heartening, so deeply encouraging as hers was to her on that day; news that drives the skeletons of the past far into the distance and transforms the things you fear in the future from demons into doorways; if you have experienced a first-hand encounter with the God who is known to turn a scar to satin and an empty shell of a heart into a vessel brimmed for pouring, then you will recall that on that day you probably left your water jar at the well too.

We have given what we have to give—our time, our attention, our study, our reflection; our efforts to pray, to love, to live fairly and faithfully. And now we are bold enough to ask

God the same—to give to us what God has to give. And God says to us. "I brought you myself. I am before you—Seeker and Sought, Caller and Called. Sighing Spirit, accompanying grace. Bread to satisfy your hungry heart. Water welling up to eternal life. Whisperer of things only true when whispered. I am before you, and I am all you need." "The gift of God," it turns out, is God.

For further reflection . . .

PART ONE

1. The precariousness of praying

Read Genesis 3. What do you think of the idea that Adam and Eve are both evasive *and* transparent, dodgy but eventually honest? Can you think of parallels in your own life, or in your experience of others?

Do you agree with the assertion that, in terms of spiritual responsibility, we sometimes claim to be "lost" when in fact we are merely "hiding"? In other words, do we sometimes claim to be on a protracted search for truth, or true community, when in fact we are merely reluctant to commit ourselves to God through an actual community of faith? Explain.

A child therapist named Garry Landreth has said, in reference to parenting, that "it's not what you do; it's what you do after what you do." How does this apply to Adam and Eve? And to our own mistakes and missteps?

Consider the claim that "the presence of God is a thing we want and ward off in just about equal measure." Do you agree or disagree? Reflect on ways that, with regard to prayer, you have behaved in one way or the other—or both.

Lord, whether we are lost, hiding, or both at once, seek us out. Call to us at a volume quiet enough for us to hear, that we and our meandering hearts may find you, and so be found. Amen.

2. Praying before we know it

Read Luke 11:1-4. In Luke's Gospel, we find Jesus at prayer from the very beginning of his ministry (e.g., 3:21, 6:12, 9:28, 10:21), but only in chapter 11 do the disciples ask him to teach them to pray. Why do you suppose this request doesn't come sooner?

In your own life, when have you delayed asking questions of deep importance? What spiritual question or questions would you ask Jesus right now if you could do so?

Sometimes we use the phrase "prevenient grace" to suggest a grace that "comes before" we are aware of our need for God. Have you ever thought about your own longing to know God as a yearning kindled by the Holy Spirit?

When faced with a difficult or trying situation, have you ever spoken words, taken action, or endured an experience beyond that which you had thought you were capable? In the wake of that event, have you had any sense of divine intervention? Explain.

An anonymous poet has written these words: "I sought the Lord, and afterward I knew / He moved my soul to seek him, seeking me." How does this poem reflect the description found in Romans 8:26 about the Spirit interceding within us?

A prayer from the same poem:

*I find, I walk, I love, but oh, the whole
Of love is but my answer, Lord, to thee!
For thou were long beforehand with my soul;
Always thou lovedst me. Amen.*

3. Embrace and surrender

Read Romans 8:22-27. Find the three uses of the word *groan* or *sigh* (the same Greek word has been translated as both). We mostly discussed in this chapter the sigh of the individual. Reflect for a moment on the idea of the sighing of the Christian community (v 23), or the sighing of creation (v 22). Imagine and describe what such a collective sigh on the part of the community might express. And the sigh of creation?

Inhale deeply, then exhale. As you do so, listen for the meanings beneath your sigh. What does that sigh call forth from your mind and heart? Of what contentedness, concern, apprehension, or other emotion does it speak?

In what ways does the matter about which you are sighing extend beyond yourself to your family? Your church family? Your community? The world?

Guided prayer: Imagine Jesus standing before a crowd, his hands outstretched in a gesture suggesting either embrace, surrender, or both. With your own hands outstretched in such a manner, reflect on this image of Jesus, then consider your own life as one of meeting the world in a posture of embrace and surrender. As you consider a certain loved one, a difficult situation in your life, a beautiful landscape, or a symphony or other work of art, let your breathing reflect that twofold action of embrace . . . surrender . . .

4. Living from elephants' tracks

Read Luke 11:1-4. What do you think of the idea that prayer can be taught by means of imitation?

Can you recall a prayer from childhood that you learned from parents, Sunday school teachers, worship gatherings, or another source?

Is there a prayer you have been taught as an adult, drawn either from a book, a hymn, a worship or study setting, or another person that you have found meaningful?

Think of persons in your life whom you esteem for their spiritual maturity. Ask them if they draw upon a certain prayer repeatedly. Is this prayer original with them, or is it drawn from another source? Begin to learn the prayer yourself.

Reflect on any tension that might exist between individual expression and creativity on the one hand and customs and community norms on the other.

Sometimes learned prayers can be adapted for a particular setting or situation. Try doing so with either of the following two prayers.

"Thank you, dear God, for this good life, and forgive us if we don't love it enough."   *Garrison Keillor*

. . . and forgive us if we don't love it enough to . . .
(Complete the sentence in your own words.)

"For all that has been, thanks. To all that will be, yes."
                                                Dag Hammarskjöld

For all that has been (_____, _____, _____), thanks.

(Include words describing events, experiences, or blessings from your own life and times.)

To all that will be (_____, _____, _____), yes. (Include words describing things you anticipate in the future.)

5. Something understood

Read Matthew 6:7-13. Notice that the Lord's Prayer follows immediately after Jesus' words of assurance that "your Father knows what you need." Identify phrases in the Lord's Prayer that confirm the truth of those words.

Now read Psalm 139:1-18. How often does the psalmist use the words "know," "search," "discern," and "acquainted" in referring to God's understanding of us? Imagine the psalmist's disposition in praying this prayer. Do you perceive contentedness? Exhilaration? Satisfaction? Do you think there may be any sense of bewilderment or exasperation woven into these other emotions?

Can you think of a time you have been seriously misunderstood? Recall the difficulty of that experience and its aftermath.

Now recall an experience in which you felt that you were thoroughly understood. Contrast the emotions accompanying this experience with those mentioned just above.

O LORD, you have searched me and known me. / You know when I sit down and when I rise up; / you discern my thoughts from far away. / You search out my path and my lying down, / and are acquainted with all my ways. / . . . Such knowledge is too wonderful for me . . .
Psalm 139

PART TWO

6. The broth of false and true

Trace the braided path of fidelity and betrayal Peter walks as you read the following passages: Mark 8:27-33; Luke 22:54-62; John 21:1-19. In what ways does Peter personify Frederick Buechner's description of the heart as "a broth of false and true"?

Imagine yourself as Peter at that charcoal fire (Luke 22:54-62). What are you feeling in the way of courage? Cowardice?

We have spoken of the hungering dark of the "belly" and the love and goodness of the sky. Real life, however, is infinitely more complex, with the belly capable of generating goodness, and the sky its own deceptions. The Greek word for "compassion," for instance, is *splanchnizomai*, from the word *splanchnon*, or gut. Have you ever felt a sense of pity or compassion welling up from the very core of your physical being? Describe that experience.

Conversely, have you ever been introduced to a lofty idea or theory that seemed enlightened and genuine but turned out to be either manipulative or deceptive? Describe such an experience.

My heart has many loves; too many for me. My heart has many loves; Love, now come and set me free. Train my heart to this truest of all affections, the love that has held me fast from before my birth, and will not ever let me go. Amen.

7. *After passion*

Read Galatians 5:16-25. Notice in verses 19-21 the wide range of attitudes and behaviors to which the phrase "passions and desires" in verse 24 refers. When we use the word *passion* in the popular sense today, we normally have other, more productive or positive meanings in mind. Even so, are there ways in which "following one's passion" can lead to some of the attitudes and behaviors identified in verse 24?

Many of my friends and colleagues believe the word *passion* has a useful and positive place in Christian vocabulary, while I see it as merely a popularized reduction of theological and vocational language, such as *purpose, guidance, calling, direction,* and *commitment.* We have benefited a great deal from discussing this question among ourselves. What are your thoughts?

"For people of faith, the difference is whether we will speak in terms of self-fulfillment or self-giving. What we know on good authority is that the latter results in what the former seeks." Do you agree with this observation? If so, how have you seen it proven true? If not, how would you restate it?

What do you think of Christopher Reeve's understanding that "I know I have to give when sometimes I really want to take"? When has this been true in your life?

Paul lists certain dispositions and behaviors that result from a decision to choose self-giving as the means to personal fulfillment, calling them "the fruit of the Spirit" (Galatians 5:22). Think of persons you know who evidence the fruit of the Spirit in their lives.

To develop Paul's metaphor, fruit is manifested only partly by effort and determination, but largely by other forces. Are there ways in which these people you have identified demonstrate an effortlessness in practicing these virtues? Are there other ways in which there is clearly effort and even struggle involved? What has been your own experience of this dynamic? Now reflect on these questions with regard to the community of faith rather than the individual.

In a way, O God, it seems as though we labor for every worthy goal and holy habit. Yet in another way, it is as though every good gift comes from beyond us, given freely from your hand. Help us, with time, to grow in the practices of our faith as fruit is grown—through persistence and patience, grit and grace, effort and ease. Amen.

8. The listening heart

Read John 14:15-27. Notice the various verbs, or actions, associated with the Advocate, the Holy Spirit: to be with you, abide with you, teach, remind. Now think of the person or persons in your life most responsible for your formation, development, and maturation into adulthood. Apply those verbs to that person. How well do they fit?

I have noted that the name *Advocate* can imply either "calling toward" or "being called toward." In terms of the person (or persons) you identified above, can you think of times when you called them to your assistance? Are there other times when they called you to partnership or responsibility?

"It is no coincidence that the word *obey* derives from the Latin 'to hear.' To yield to God's larger purposes is to begin to have the ear opened to God's specific guidance for our own lives." How have you found this so in your life? Are there ways in which you would disagree with this notion? Explain.

We often hear about "God's will" as a personal reference, as though God had a separately plotted course for every individual to follow through life. What if we were to think instead of God's will as a more overarching set of behaviors and purposes, within which one's own sense of vocation comes to fruition? Would you find that a helpful way to think about God's will? Why or why not?

Order our steps to follow goodness and mercy, O God, trusting that surely goodness and mercy will follow us, too, all the days of our lives. Amen.

9. Whispering in church

Read Psalm 96. Subtitled in my Bible "Praise to God Who Comes in Judgment," notice how this psalm never addresses God directly. Rather, every verse encourages the faith community in its praise. Such "horizontal prayer" is a common pattern in the Psalter. Do you find this surprising or reasonable? How so?

What do you think of the notion that God's people gathered in worship are schooling one another even as we worship, that our praise is meant to be heard as much horizontally as vertically?

". . . The experience of the Christian community's holy indifference to my heart's whims, coupled with an utmost concern for its well-being, is one of the greatest gifts we'll ever receive in life." Can you think of examples in your life or others' situations in which indifference and concern worked together over time in the practice of love?

"I never cease to be amazed how often the meat and bread of God's communications are borne on a raven's wing rather than an angel's." To better understand this reference, read 1 Kings 17:1-7. Why do you suppose God so often prefers "ravens" or their equivalent to more angelic messengers?

If I were to ask whether the church were more like a raven or an angel, your answer might change depending on the day! Given the mixed nature of the church's composition and its mixed record of fidelity to its purpose, do you find anything hopeful in knowing that God has always worked in "mixed media" to accomplish God's aims? Explain.

Reflecting on the "mix" that you yourself represent, how do you regard your own acceptance by the church and your role within its common life?

Lead me, Lord: to join in the whispering of the church, lead me; to experience and practice the love that blends holy indifference and utmost concern, lead me; to heed the call that begins at the font, and echoes far beyond, lead me. Then I shall know your will for my life, and for our life together. Amen.

10. The power of our reluctance

Read Matthew 21:28-32. This parable, as well as the question and exhortation that follow, is addressed to chief priests and elders who have been challenging Jesus in the temple. Hidden within this testy dialogue between religious power brokers and Jesus is good news: there is a group—represented by "the tax collectors and the prostitutes"—that first rejected God or renounced faith, then returned to the fold. These "late-hour" believers will be accepted in God's sight before those who used to believe and continue to say they believe (certain chief priests and elders), but who are not responding to the moment at hand.

Do you believe, as Jesus (and his opponents) did, that a "no" followed by compliance is better than a "yes" followed by dismissal? Why or why not?

Reflect on E. Stanley Jones's observation that antitheses strongly marked are a part of what makes a person strong. How is it that a complex perspective on life and faith could be stronger than a simple viewing of life and faith in a single dimension?

Can you recall a time when you have struggled with a decision, saying "no" at first before ever saying "yes"? Was there a "John" figure who helped you toward that eventual leap of faith? Are there roles of serving or leading that you currently fill in which you continue to struggle, as Jeremiah and Jonah did? Are there others who may struggle in their vocational roles for whom you may be a "John" figure?

We have learned since Mother Teresa's death that she struggled deeply with her vocational work. How does this information affect the way you regard her life of service? Is there any sense in which this added perspective lends encouragement for our own leading and serving roles?

Make me a captive, Lord,
And then I shall be free;
Force me to render up my sword,
And I shall conqueror be.
I sink in life's alarms
When by myself I stand;
Imprison me within thine arms,
And strong shall be my hand. Amen.

George Matheson, 1842–1906

PART THREE

11. The sincerity of the Messiah

Read Matthew 12:9-21. Focus for the present on Matthew's reference to Isaiah in verses 17-21 as a means of illuminating Jesus' way of being in ministry. What do we learn from these words, spoken by the divine through the prophet Isaiah, about the character of "my servant"?

Notice some of the contrasts or paradoxes in this portrayal:

- the God of Israel has chosen him, is pleased with him, and has put his Spirit upon him; yet he is sent to the Gentiles;
- he will proclaim justice, but he will not cry aloud;
- finally, he will bring justice, but he will not break a bruised reed or quench a smoldering wick in order to do so.

Consider the middle contrast above. How does a leader, or a leading community within society, such as the church, make something heard, particularly something of such significance as justice, without shouting?

Now look at the final contrast. Can you imagine the process of establishing justice in such a peaceable way? What are some examples of how this might occur?

What are your initial reactions to labeling Jesus as "sincere"? Why do you suppose this word has sometimes been understood pejoratively in our culture? Have you ever been in a situation in which you were especially relieved that the person relating to you was sincere? Explain.

God of justice and peace, how can you possibly accomplish both of these at once? How, in a whisper, shall we ever be a witness, heard beneath the deafening din of violence and powermongering? Against all odds, may we be heard in the same manner by which your servant Jesus was also heard in his day, and continues to be heard in ours, that is, by the miracle of your grace. Amen.

12. Two hands

Read Philippians 3:7-14. In verse 13, Paul writes that "this one thing I do," identifying that one thing in verse 14. What is the "one thing" the apostle Paul does? What sort of "clearing the deck" does he do in order to focus on that one thing? (See verse 14b.)

The question of "the one thing" most important to a life, a group, a community, or an institution, often calls for hours of reflection and examination on the part of those who take it seriously. Sometimes this exercise of discerning a central purpose for one's life is undertaken repeatedly over the years, with former outcomes being revised or even dismissed in the process. If you were to say the "one thing" that matters most in your life, how would you describe what that one thing is—the goal toward which everything you are and do is focused? Do your life and lifestyle reflect that priority? Now ask these questions from the standpoint of your family, then that of your church family.

Even before we learned to walk and chew gum at the same time, multitasking has been a normal part of human existence. We breathe while we sing, dream while we sleep, think while we listen, whistle while we work, and so on. Multitasking behavior is more of a continuum than an on-off switch, benefiting us in many ways when practiced appropriately, but also capable of interfering with the act of being fully present to a specific task, situation, person, or experience.

Where do you place yourself on the multitasking continuum, in terms of day-to-day tendencies and demands? What would be involved in deciding to move along that continuum in the direction of greater simplicity of tasks, of "doing what you are doing"? What would be some of the benefits to you and those around you?

What might be a negative effect of your doing fewer things at once? How would you compare or balance the two different outcomes?

While considering the season of "Ordinary Time" in the Christian year, I write that "Wide open spaces on the sacred calendar serve to remind us that there are also, if we allow it to be so, wide open spaces in the mind and heart." What would you say is the importance of having such wide open spaces in the mind and heart? And what about in the life of the Christian community?

Philip Simmons has written that "the present moment, like the spotted owl or the sea turtle, has become an endangered species." Do you agree? Why or why not?

Take my hands and let them move at the impulse of thy love.
Frances R. Havergal

13. A cantilevered life

Read Romans 10:14-15. Notice the logical progression of verbs set into the sequence of four questions in these two verses: to call on, to believe, to hear, to proclaim, to be sent. Then a leap occurs as Paul quotes Isaiah on the subject of feet: "How beautiful are the feet of those who bring good news!" In an instant, Paul has moved from the field of ideas—hearing, sharing, experiencing, believing—to the field itself: the traveling feet that make these things possible. He has employed what is known as a synecdoche—a literary device in which the part (the feet) represents the whole (the person and their calling)—to celebrate the courage and beauty of one who "steps out" in faith to bring good news to others.

"When someone brings good news at a moment we most desperately need it, everything about them—feet, nose, pointy ears—becomes instantly and for all time beautiful." Have you ever had such an experience? Conversely, have you ever been gazed upon in such a way, having been the one who brought grace, comfort, good news, or assurance to another in a time of acute need?

William Sloane Coffin has made this observation: "I love the recklessness of faith. First you leap; then you grow wings." As you ponder this idea, does it leave you feeling more of a sense of exhilaration or apprehension? Explain.

O God, may every step I take today, including this very prayer, be its own small leap of faith. Let me be so grounded in the awareness of your love and provision that my heart and hands reach toward every needed place, and upward in praise and thanksgiving, not hindered by fear of falling, but freely and with joy. If in this trust walk I cannot always be certain of my way, then let me be assured of your presence. May I see in every surrendering step your gift to me, and mine to you, of this cantilevered life. Amen.

14. The whisper beneath the shout

Read Luke 3:1-18. Note how titles are raised like banners in the beginning verses of this text. Everyone has a designation, an office, a jurisdiction. Everyone, that is, but John, who is identified only as someone's kid, and as residing in some no-name wilderness. Now notice, in the grand parade of introductions, the one to whom the word of God comes. What does Luke seem to be saying here, in the words beneath the words, by the way in which he bypasses the landed and legitimized to home in on a virtual nobody for the purpose of carrying his narrative forward?

Isaiah was speaking of geography when he envisioned the re-working of terrain for the sake of preparing for royal travel. Based on the dialogue between John and the crowd that follows the quote from Isaiah (vv 4-6), do you suppose Luke had reworking of another sort in mind? Explain.

Based on your experience, in what ways have toy drives and similar expressions of care during the Christmas season brought a sense of mutual joy and fulfillment on the part of both giver and recipient? Are there other ways in which these efforts seem to have missed John's message of sharing and sacrifice?

What would it mean for you to follow John's advice in a concrete and tangible way, bringing a contribution to the food/toy/blanket drive directly from home rather than from the grocery store or mall? Beyond being an interesting idea to ponder or activity to practice, does such a consideration raise for you any deeper questions concerning lifestyle or discipleship?

Imagine yourself among the crowds that came out to hear John in the wilderness. Now listen closely to yourself as you verbalize their question on your own lips: "What should we do?" What do you hear being expressed in your tone of voice? Is there weariness? Hopefulness? Indifference? Eagerness? Some other emotion?

Lord, the wilderness in which John resides could, at times, be my own heart, or our own society. What should we do? How should we respond? What fruits can we bear that have the mark of true change? If valleys are to be raised in us, and rough places made plain, remind us of that which brought us to John's wilderness—our own wilderness—in the first place: the longing to know and follow you. Amen.

15. Will work for food

Read John 6:22-35.

"With the pairing of two sorts of 'food' in the same sentence, Jesus provides us with a keen insight into human nature: there's a hunger in the heart that is so closely bound up, body and soul, with other hungers that we often confuse them." Can you identify examples of this confusion of hungers? How can we grow more aware of the difference between spiritual and physical hungers, as well as more careful in responding to each appropriately?

Barbara Kingsolver has observed that the average American consumes enough food to support thirty citizens of India, a claim we can surely believe when we review the lifetime food consumption inventory for a typical American. Did anything in the inventory of lifetime food consumption especially surprise you? To which categories are you most fond of contributing? Are there certain food groups that deserve less of your attention than you give them?

Every day around the world 35,000 children die of hunger-related and other preventable causes, while we in this country discard enough food each day to feed many times that number. The amount Americans spend annually to feed our pets exceeds by billions of dollars what it would cost to feed the human beings around the globe who are left to hunger. What are some ways the Christian community can work to overcome the disconnect between these realities? What action can you take in that effort, both in terms of lifestyle and witness?

God of every good harvest, help us share with generosity from harvests with which we are best acquainted, and receive with gratitude from harvests to which we are largely strangers. Jesus, bread of life, too often we would seek you for what you hold for us in your hand rather than for what you see in us with your eye; help us heed your invitation to be nourished first and foremost through friendship with you. Holy Spirit, giver of life, deliver us from appetites that deaden rather than satisfy; open our lives to sharing in your mystery of love and purpose, and so make us and all your creation truly alive. Amen.